INSIGHT POCKET GUIDE

Mal[

APA PUBLICATIONS
Part of the Langenscheidt Publishing Group

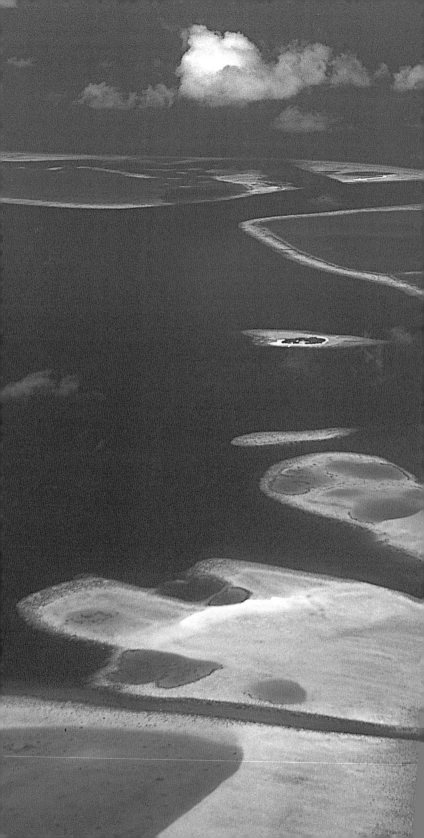

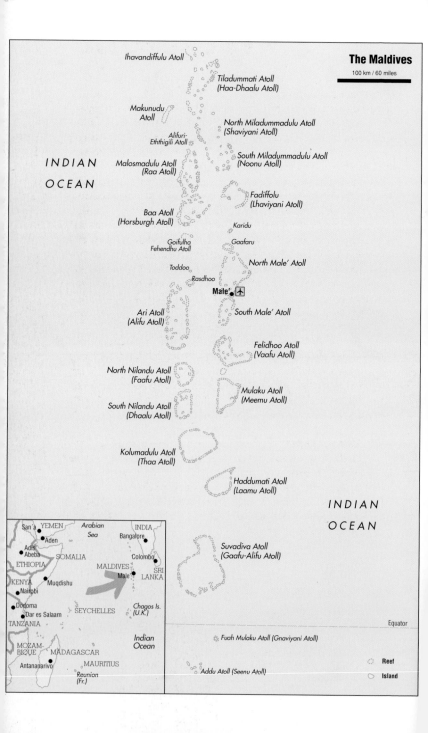

The Maldives

100 km / 60 miles

Ihavandiffulu Atoll

Tiladummati Atoll (Haa-Dhaalu Atoll)

Makunudu Atoll

North Miladummadulu Atoll (Shaviyani Atoll)

Alifuri-Eththigili Atoll

South Miladummadulu Atoll (Noonu Atoll)

INDIAN

Malosmadulu Atoll (Raa Atoll)

OCEAN

Fadiffolu (Lhaviyani Atoll)

Baa Atoll (Horsburgh Atoll)

Karidu

Goifulha Fehendhu Atoll

Gaafaru

Toddoo

North Male' Atoll

Rasdhoo

Male' ✈

Ari Atoll (Alifu Atoll)

South Male' Atoll

Felidhoo Atoll (Vaafu Atoll)

North Nilandu Atoll (Faafu Atoll)

Mulaku Atoll (Meemu Atoll)

South Nilandu Atoll (Dhaalu Atoll)

Kolumadulu Atoll (Thaa Atoll)

Haddumati Atoll (Laamu Atoll)

INDIAN

OCEAN

Suvadiva Atoll (Gaafu-Alifu Atoll)

San'a YEMEN *Arabian Sea* INDIA

Aden Bangalore

Adis Abeba

ETHIOPIA SOMALIA Colombo

MALDIVES SRI

KENYA Male' LANKA

Muqdishu

Nairobi

Dodoma *Chagos Is. (U.K.)*

Dar es Salaam SEYCHELLES

TANZANIA *Indian Ocean*

Equator

MOZAM-BIQUE MADAGASCAR

MAURITIUS

Antananarivo

Reunion (Fr.)

🌸 *Fuah Mulaku Atoll (Gnaviyani Atoll)*

🪸 **Reef**

🪸 *Addu Atoll (Seenu Atoll)*

◯ **Island**

Welcome

This book combines the interests and enthusiasms of two of the world's best-known information providers: Insight Guides, who have set the standard for visual travel guides since 1970, and Discovery Channel, the world's premier source of non-fiction television programming. Written by Insight's Maldives correspondents Shoo-Yin Lim and Denise Nielsen Tackett, it aims to bring you the best of the Maldives.

The ultimate sensual crescent of white sand and turquoise sea: a description that fits like a glove when describing the beaches of the Maldivian atolls. There are no great cities or historical monuments to visit, yet every year, more than 400,000 visitors come in search of paradise lost – that and the most superlative diving found in the Indian Ocean. In this book are recommendations of resorts that span a range of prices and levels of luxury – a prime consideration in this mostly one-island, one-resort destination. Also included is a walking tour of the capital, Male', and sections on history and culture, diving and dive sites, shopping and food, water sports and other leisure activities, plus a useful practical information section covering transport, money matters and other travel know-how.

Shoo-Yin Lim is a Singapore-based writer and film director who returns to the Maldives whenever she feels homesick for sand and sea, something which happens with alarming frequency. She first visited the Maldives way back in 1985, and to this day recommends its paradise islands as a surefire antidote to the stresses of urban life.

Denise Nielsen Tackett, an American marine researcher, and freelance writer and photographer, spent three fruitful years in the Maldives. Underwater, she was enthralled by the variety and concentration of marine life, having done close to 1,000 dives in these waters. On land, she is thankful for time spent with the gentle, warm-hearted Maldivians who opened up their homes and lives to her.

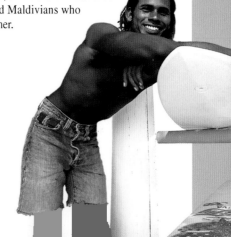

BAA ATOLL

EXCURSIONS

DIVING

DIVE SITES

LEISURE ACTIVITIES

PRACTICAL INFORMATION

MAPS

CREDITS AND INDEX

Pages 2/3: aerial view of Maldivian reefs
Pages 8/9: a school of orange basslets

History & Culture

Hanging like a garland below the southern tip of India are the 1,190 tropical islands that make up the Maldives. Although not the smallest nation in the world, this is certainly the most watery, with the sea representing 99 percent of its territory. For the many visitors who make it to these shores, the appeal of these quintessential tropical islands lies not in the historical, but the natural – soft white sands, swaying palms and transparent waters teeming with marine life are the biggest draws.

Early Origins

Strategically located at the crossroads of major East-West trade routes, the Maldives was a familiar port-of-call for many early seafaring civilisations. Reference to the islands is first found in the work of Ptolemy, the Greek geographer, in AD 2. The archipelago appears again in the late 4th century works of Pappus of Alexandria and Scholasticus, a Theban who mentioned the many islands and their dangerous reefs that attracted unwary ships.

In the 9th and 10th centuries, Persian and Arab travellers mention the queens who ruled these islands, and the local abundance of cowries (small shells used as money). For centuries, the Maldives was known as the centre of the cowrie trade. Today, two small cowries appear in the corner of all Maldivian bank notes, a tribute to their former importance to this island state.

The Maldives was known to the Chinese as the 'submerged Liu mountains' by the time of the Ming Dynasty (1368–1644). On an expedition to East Africa in 1433, explorer Ma Huan referred to the islands as a supplier of rope to seafarers, and he writes that they are the 'weak waters' referred to in the 5th century BC Chinese *Classic History*. The islands had become prosperous through trading by the time Vasco da Gama opened up the Indian Ocean to Portuguese influence in 1498.

Because of their location, the islands attracted seafarers, both by intention and shipwreck, from many places, including Malaysia, Indonesia, Egypt, Greece and what was Arabia and the Roman Empire, as well as from India and Sri Lanka. Archaeological expeditions, led by British archaeologist H.C.P. Bell in the 1920s and by Norwegian explorer Thor Heyerdahl in the 1980s, uncovered evidence to suggest that Buddhism and Hinduism had arrived here by 500 BC. Among the most revealing of Bell's findings were Buddhist manuscripts and the head of a Buddha statue dating from the 11th century.

Heyerdahl's research also led him to theorise that the Maldives was inhabited as early as 2000 BC by a people he called the Redin. Little is known about these Redin but archaeologists have uncovered evidence which

Left: a pre-Islamic Maldivian sculpture
Right: Portuguese explorer Vasco da Gama (c.1469–1524)

indicates that they were sun worshippers and built large temples facing the east. They left behind images, and texts in a script similar to that of an ancient Indus valley civilisation. The Redin temples were destroyed as Buddhism gradually supplanted the ancient religion of sun worship. Reconstructed as Buddhist temples, these structures were once again demolished to make way for mosques after the conversion to Islam in AD 1153.

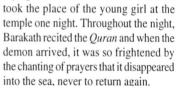

The language used on the islands is called Dhivehi, and the Maldivians themselves are Dhivehin, and their country *Dhivehi Raaje* (realm of the Dhivehin). Dhivehi is an Indo-Aryan language with influences from Sinhala, Hindi, Arabic and Bengali, although its development, since it was spoken by isolated islanders, was independent of the mainstream. It is written from right to left in a script that is unique to the Maldives, called *Thaana*. The word 'Maldives' itself probably came from the Sanskrit word *Maladeepa*, meaning 'garland of islands'. Like their language, which reflects the influence of the ancient seafarers, Maldivians today are a mixed race.

Conversion to Islam

Although its strategic position exposed the Maldives to many seafaring cultures, it is the Arabs who had the most influence on these islands. They were responsible for the most significant event in the islands' history – the introduction of Islam in AD 1153. The Islamic conversion is recounted in a well-known legend by the Arab traveller Ibn Battuta. The story goes that the sea-demon Rannamari had been terrorising the people of Male', the present capital of the Maldives. In order to appease the demon, the natives sacrificed a young virgin at the temple each month. A Moroccan traveller by the name of Abu'al Barakath who was staying in Male' learnt of the demon and

took the place of the young girl at the temple one night. Throughout the night, Barakath recited the *Quran* and when the demon arrived, it was so frightened by the chanting of prayers that it disappeared into the sea, never to return again.

Whatever the veracity of the story, the Maldivian King Kalaminja was so impressed that he embraced Islam and declared it the national religion. To this day, Barakath is much venerated, and his tomb stands in Male' as a holy shrine.

Colonial Encounters

After the adoption of Islam in 1153, three sultanic dynasties – which included three female rulers – ruled the country peacefully for the next 400 years. In 1517, Sul-

Above: Arab sailors on the Indian Ocean
Left: detail of a mosque door in Male'

tan Kalu Muhammad signed a treaty with the Portuguese, allowing them to establish an unpopular trading post in Male'. With the help of some Indian corsairs, the Maldivians succeeded in destroying the post, only to have the Portuguese retaliate by sending a small armada to build a fort there instead.

The next sultan, Hassan IX, was influenced by the Portuguese and converted to Christianity while on a trip to India. His efforts to convert key Maldivians to Christianity in 1552 failed when his sympathisers were seized. This incurred the wrath of the Portuguese, and in 1558, Captain Andreas Andre invaded the Maldives. The occupation lasted for 15 years and was marked by brutality, despair and an on-going guerrilla war. The Portuguese were finally ousted in 1573 when three brothers from Utheemu island led a rebellion and killed the whole garrison – shortly before the deadline for Maldivians to convert to Christianity or face certain death. Muhammed Thakurufaanu, one of the brothers who led the rebellion, became the next sultan and introduced many reforms, including the minting of coins and the establishment of a militia. The Maldives has not been ruled by a foreign power since, and today Thakurufaanu is regarded as the greatest national hero.

In 1645, diplomatic ties were established with the Dutch, who had ousted the Portuguese as the dominant power in the Indian Ocean. In exchange for cowries, the islands received supplies of spices, areca nuts and ammunition. In 1752–3, a small expedition headed by Ali Raja from south India tried to invade the Maldives but was repelled with the help of a small French fleet.

From Sultanate to Republic

When the British chased the Dutch from Ceylon (now Sri Lanka) in 1796, the sultans in the Maldives maintained cordial relations with the new colonial power. By 1887 the relationship was defined and letters were exchanged between the governor of Ceylon, representing Britain, and Sultan Mohamed Mueendudden II of the Maldives.

The relationship was uneasy, but it enabled the Maldives to enjoy the status of a protected state, without actually

being a Protectorate. There was no British representative based on the islands, and Britain had no power to interfere in internal matters. Yet it was at their behest that the first of several constitutions was adopted in 1932, following which Hassan Nooraddeen II became the first elected sultan.

Ten years later, the constitution was rewritten, but the elected sultan declined to serve. Prime Minister Muhammed Amin Didi took over and started a modernisation programme which led to the establishment of the forerunner of the present National Security Service and the nationalisation of fish exports. The Sultanate was abolished in 1953 and Amin Didi became the country's first president. Food shortages, a ban on tobacco and riots led to his downfall and the demise of the constitution. In 1954, Muhammed Farid Didi took the throne as the last sultan.

Above: an 1886 newspaper article

With Ceylon's independence from Britain in 1948, a new agreement was signed giving Britain control of Maldivian foreign affairs while the Maldives maintained control of its domestic affairs. During World War II the British had built airstrips on Gan and Kela islands to protect their interests. Many Maldivians were employed at the Gan airstrip, and in 1956 the British were granted a 100-year lease on it. The following year, the newly elected President Ibrahim Nasir revoked the lease, unleashing a revolt in the southernmost atolls. In 1959, the three southern atolls seceded from the Maldives and formed the

United Suvadive Islands, prompting Nasir to re-negotiate the air-base lease with the British. By 1963, the atolls were again part of the Maldives, and independence from British representation was discussed. On 26 July 1965, the Maldives became an independent nation and joined the United Nations. Three years later, a new constitution was drawn up and the Maldives became a republic with Nasir as president.

By 1972, the constitution had been amended to increase the president's powers. The same year, currency controls instituted by Sri Lanka caused the collapse of the dried fish market – the Maldives' biggest export. Fortunately for the islands, tourism arrived with the opening of the first two resorts. However, the benefits from the new industry did not filter down to the ordinary people. Accused of appropriating government funds, Nasir fled the country in 1978. Over the years, he had siphoned off a large part of the Maldives treasury.

In 1978, Maumoon Abdul Gayoom was elected president, and he has been re-elected four times since, most recently in 1998. Along the way, his regime has survived three attempted coups, in 1980, 1981 and 1988. Gayoom has been credited with significantly improving the standard of living throughout the country, especially in health, education, communications and environmental conservation. His championing of ecological causes and issues of relevance to small island states has earned international recognition for the Maldives.

Governing by Faith

The Maldives is a Muslim country and its inhabitants are all Sunni Muslims of the Shafi'ite sect, one of the most liberal of all Islamic groups. Life and religion are completely integrated and the Islamic law is the law of the land. The five pillars of Islam are adhered to throughout the islands: the affirmation that 'there is no God but God and Mohammed is His prophet'; prayer five times a day; alms-giving; dawn-to-sundown fasting during the month of *Ramadan*; and if possible, a pilgrimage to Mecca.

From a very young age, the Maldivian learns the fundamentals of Islam and recites the *Quran*. On Fridays, the men don their best for the *hukuru namaad,* or Friday prayers, to reaffirm their faith in Allah, while the women pray in separate mosques or at home. The consumption of pork and alcohol are prohibited. Fasting during *Ramadan* is strictly observed and working hours are rescheduled to accommodate this difficult period.

Above: Muhammed Amin Didi, the country's first president

The practice of Islam is relatively liberal in this island nation. The Maldives is governed by Islamic law, or *shari'a*, but maximum punishments are usually not meted out. The usual sentence is banishment to another atoll for a period of time – the rationale being that there is no worse punishment than separation from family and friends. For crimes of adultery and alcohol consumption, a mild form of flogging is added to the banishment – more to make an example of the person than to hurt him.

Divorces are easy to obtain and many Maldivians joke, though not uncomfortably, about the country's high divorce rate. Despite this, no stigma is attached to divorce, perhaps because it is a carry-over from the days of old when seafarers would stop here, take a temporary wife and then divorce her before setting sail again. Today's younger generation is more inclined to choose a mate for life, perhaps because life is not as transient as it once was.

Despite their strong faith, some Maldivians are traditionally superstitious and believe in *dhevi*, supernatural spirits that dwell in the natural surroundings. Recitations from the *Quran*, potions and spells from a *hakeem*, or medicine man, are used to drive them away.

Maldivian Dance

Bodu beru, or big drum, is the most popular form of traditional entertainment in the Maldives. The drum is made from a hollowed-out coconut tree, covered in goatskin (or, more often today, the sail from windsurfing boards) and held together by a coir rope. *Bodu beru* is performed by two or three drummers, a singer and a chorus, with all the men, and sometimes women, joining in to dance. There is a fine tradition of male dancing on the islands, and the *bodu beru* is encouraged as a form of creative expression.

Above: old and new minarets in Male'
Right: frenetic beating of the *bodu beru*

The spirited music accompanying the *bodu beru* starts off with a slow beat and gradually works up to a frenetic pace. The loud, rhythmic beat encourages more dancers to join in as the pace picks up. *Bodu beru* originated decades ago when seafarers from Africa, Arabia and Indonesia stopped here on their voyages and shared their song and dance customs with the Maldivians. Over time, the meaning of the song lyrics has been lost, but the spirit of the music remains. *Bodu beru* performances can be seen at some resorts, which organise weekly cultural performances for guests.

Other less common dances include *tharaa*, or tambourine, a dance introduced by the Gulf Arabs, and *dhanndhi jehun*, both performed by men only. The *bandiyaa jehun* is an adaptation of the Indian pot dance, performed only by young women, in which the dancers beat their fingers against the metal water pots they carry. It was once popular on Toddoo, an island north of Ari Atoll.

Living with Nature

While the sea provides Maldivians with food, shelter and jobs – fishing accounts for more than 70 percent of total exports – it also wreaks havoc on these small, exposed islands. Fierce storms and tidal swells occur frequently throughout the country. In 1987, a huge tidal swell covered parts of Male' and swamped huge areas of newly reclaimed land. Many islands, including the airport, were flooded and damage was substantial. In an effort to protect the island from future tidal swells, a breakwater, consisting of 20,000 three-ton cement tetrapods, was constructed along the south side of Male'.

But even that may not be enough to save the Maldives if environmentalists are correct in their predictions of global warming; as most of the islands are less than 2 metres (6½ ft) above sea level, even a small rise in the ocean will inundate hundreds of them. Some scientists speculate that at the present rate of sea-level rise, the Maldives could be completely wiped out as early as 2100.

The global warming issue is further exacerbated by the practice of indiscriminate coral mining. For years, coral has been harvested from the shallow reefs for use as building material. Pressure from the increasing population and a new affluence among Maldivians has led to an increased demand for mined coral for new houses and buildings. Realising the folly of mining the fringing reefs which protect the islands from the pounding surf, the government has set aside certain reefs for mining and is assessing penalties for those who are caught mining outside the designated areas.

At international environmental conferences, President Gayoom has been especially vocal in bringing the plight of low-lying island countries to the attention of the developed world. The United Nations has come to the Maldives' assistance, and with their help the government has developed a National Action Plan to try to manage the local environment.

Above: illegal coral mining

HISTORY HIGHLIGHTS

history/culture

1153 King Kalaminja declares Islam the national religion.

1343 The Theemuge dynasty is replaced by the Veeru Umaru dynasty.

1517 The Portuguese establish a trading post in Male'.

1558 The Portuguese, led by Capt Andreas Andre, invade the Maldives. Andre tries to convert Maldivians to Christianity.

1573 The Portuguese are ousted in a rebellion. Militia established and first coins minted.

1602 Frenchman Francois Pyrard de Laval is shipwrecked and taken prisoner for five years. He later publishes a three-volume account of his observations in the Maldives.

1645 The islands make diplomatic contacts with the Dutch colony in Ceylon.

1796 The British take over from the Dutch in Ceylon. Trade between Male' and Colombo increases.

1879 H.C.P. Bell investigates a shipwreck in the Maldives.

1887 Britain, through its government in Ceylon, becomes responsible for foreign affairs in the Maldives.

1906 First post office opens.

1920 H.C.P. Bell returns to carry out archaeological excavations.

1932 The first written constitution is drawn up.

1942 The British establish two airstrips during World War II.

1943 Sultan Abdul Majeed Didi abdicates. Amin Didi assumes power. The National Security Service is set up and fish exports are nationalised.

1948 A mutual defence pact is signed with the British.

1953 The Sultanate is abolished. Amin Didi becomes President of the First Republic.

1954 Sultanate reinstated. Last sultan takes the throne.

1956 The British negotiate a 100-year lease on their air base on Gan island.

1957 Ibrahim Nasir is elected president. His call for a review of the British occupation of Gan leads to three southern atolls breaking away to form a separate state called United Suvadive Islands.

1960 The Maldives grants the British a 30-year lease of Gan.

1962 The break away atolls become part of the Maldives again.

1965 On 26 July, British relinquish their role. The Maldives becomes fully independent and joins the UN.

1968 Sultanate is abolished and republican constitution is adopted. Nasir becomes President of the Second Republic.

1972 Market for dried fish collapses. First two resorts open.

1978 Nasir flees to Singapore having transferred over months a huge part of the government's coffer. Maumoon Abdul Gayoom is elected president.

1981–82 Male' airport is built.

1982 Thor Heyerdahl begins excavations in southern atolls.

1983 The Maldives is made a special member of the Commonwealth of Nations. Gayoom is re-elected.

1985 Meeting of Commonwealth Finance Ministers.

1987 Tidal swell causes flooding and beach erosion throughout the islands.

1988 Gayoom is re-elected for a third term. A third coup is foiled.

1990 The Maldives celebrates 25 years of independence. Breakwater on south side of Male' is completed.

1992 Adopted as the SAARC (South Asian Association of Regional Cooperation) Year of the Environment. Maldives participates in the Earth Summit at Rio de Janerio.

1997 The 'Visit Maldives' campaign is launched.

1998 Gayoom is elected for a fifth term. Tourism is further expanded with 14 new resorts.

Resorts

The vast majority of visitors to the Maldives stay at all-inclusive resorts built on previously uninhabited islands. This is part of a national policy of providing the best custom-made facilities for tourists without disrupting the traditional island lifestyle of the Maldivians. With only 200 islands classified as inhabited, there are nearly 1,000 others, of which 87 have become holiday resorts, with more planned for development.

Each resort island houses only one resort, with the exception of the large island of Kuramathi, which has three resorts, all run by the same management. There is one resort (Equatorial Village, on Gan island) that has causeway access to neighbouring inhabited islands. However, it is not permitted for any tourists to stay overnight on the inhabited islands, except on the capital island of Male', where there are several small hotels.

The independent tourist is therefore a very rare sight, and the majority of visitors arrive on package holidays. Most visitors are from Europe, with more Britons than any other nationality, followed by Germans and Italians. Recently the islands have gained in popularity with the Japanese and Australians.

Accommodation and Facilities

Room rates vary greatly among the resorts, and from season to season. During the high season, from December to April, the double-room full-board price is US$150–US$700 per night. Older, smaller resorts with basic facilities cater for the lower-budget traveller, while brand-name resorts with individual villas and every conceivable luxury are in the top bracket. Medium-range resorts are often better value than higher-priced ones since they are more established and so offer better service and more dining options.

In general, accommodation is either in semi-detached bungalows with thatched or tiled roofs, or in terraced blocks with a fine stretch of beach in front. All resorts have desalination plants providing fresh water for their bathrooms, private generators and scientific waste-disposal methods.

The past few years have seen a great deal of upgrading at many resorts. Air-conditioning, mini-bars, direct-dial telephones and even television have become standard fixtures at some resorts. In the more sophisticated resorts you will find fresh-water pools, spas, Jacuzzis, tennis courts and gymnasiums.

Most tour packages include transfers between airport and resort, accommodation and meals, either on a bed-and-breakfast, half-board or full-board basis. Some also have all-inclusive rates, which include drinks. Some resorts have only one restaurant and only take full-board package guests. Menu choice at such resorts is limited, with most meals being served as buffets.

Left: an idyllic resort beach, shaded by palms
Right: enjoying the glorious weather

There is little possibility of going to another resort for a meal. However, larger resorts, especially those with bed-and-breakfast rates, have snack bars, speciality restaurants and beach-grill dining. All resorts have well-stocked bars, although no alcohol is sold in Male'. And every resort has a gift shop with a range of beachwear and essentials. Nightly entertainment is usually an occasional disco, live band or Maldivian cultural show.

Choosing a Resort

Resorts are generally booked from home, and the choice is governed by what your travel agent can offer. Rooms at some resorts are committed to specific tour operators catering to a particular nationality and have, for example, German-only or Italian-only guests. There are also tour operators based in the Maldives (*see page 90*) who can arrange accommodation for independent travellers. Holidays can also be booked on the Internet. Remember that low season rates can be up to 50 percent cheaper than in high season.

Because of the distance between Ari and Baa atolls from Male', the only way to get to these atolls is to fly by seaplane, adding measurably to the cost of a holiday since domestic flights in the Maldives are expensive. Bear in mind also that if your international flight arrives at night in Male' and you're heading to Ari or Baa atoll, you have to spend the night in Male' and catch a seaplane the following morning (seaplanes are only allowed to operate during daylight hours, whereas boats operate throughout the night).

Your choice of resort will also be governed by what you want to do. For lots of activity, choose a large resort; for tranquillity, pick a resort that is more exclusive. If you plan to do a lot of snorkelling, check if the resort has a good 'house reef' – a reef close to the beach. No matter where you choose

to stay, you can be certain of lots of sunshine, sandy beaches washed by a clear lagoon and stunning marine life. And keep in mind the house rules: no nude bathing, no picking of coral from the reefs, and no fishing on the house reefs.

The resorts below will appeal to most visitors. Others of note are listed on pages 83–8. When the island name differs from that of the resort, it is indicated in brackets. Price ranges here are for a standard double room (with full board, unless otherwise stated) per night in high season:

$ = under US$150; $$ = US$151–US$200; $$$ = US$201–US$250; $$$$ = US$251–US$400; $$$$$ = above US$400

Above: night-time entertainment at Baros
Left: staff at the resorts are invariably friendly

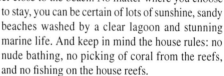

North
Male' Atoll

1. KURUMBA VILLAGE (VIHAMANA FUSHI)
(see map, p22)

No of rooms: 171; Distance from airport: 3 km (2 miles); Price range: $$$; Local agent: Universal Enterprises, 39 Orchid Magu, Male', tel: 32-3080, fax: 32-0274; Resort tel: 44-2324, fax: 44-3885, e-mail: kurumba@ dhivehinet.net.mv, web: www.unisurf.com

The Maldives' first resort opened on the island of Vihamana Fushi in 1972. Kurumba (meaning 'young coconut') is the closest resort to Male' and is ideal for travellers wishing to mix business with pleasure. There is a convention centre for 500 guests and a fully equipped business centre. The resort has a large fleet of speedboats for hire, providing quick and efficient, though expensive, transfers to and from Male' in less than 10 minutes.

The 1½-km (1-mile) long island is beautifully landscaped with hibiscus and bougainvillea shrubs, and frangipani and coconut trees. Over the years the resort has undergone substantial upgrading. The rooms and suites are tastefully furnished, with all the necessary mod cons like air-conditioning, hot and cold baths, hairdryers, direct-dial telephones and mini-bars.

While food and its lack of variety is a common complaint at many resorts, Kurumba Village prides itself on having five restaurants which offer several types of cuisine. Guests from Male' and other resorts sometimes hop over to Kurumba for a Chinese dinner at the Ming Court or a North Indian meal at the Kurumba Mahal. Besides the main restaurant and an upmarket continental restaurant, there is also a 24-hour coffee house. A favourite is the open-air terrace where you can enjoy fresh Maldivian lobsters while your toes dig into the sand under the starlit sky. A nightly disco offers after-dinner entertainment, and there is also a piano and karaoke bar.

The resort has a full list of sports facilities such as windsurfing, water-skiing, snorkelling, night fishing and a glass-bottom boat to explore the reefs around the island. The diving school is run by Eurodivers, one of the biggest dive operators in the islands. In addition, there is a fitness centre, two swimming pools, two floodlit tennis courts and a billiard room. There is also the Harmony Centre for natural therapies.

Kurumba has matured over the years into the 'grand hotel' of the Maldives, with high standards that result in a value-for-money, top-class resort.

Right: the main swimming pool at Kurumba Village

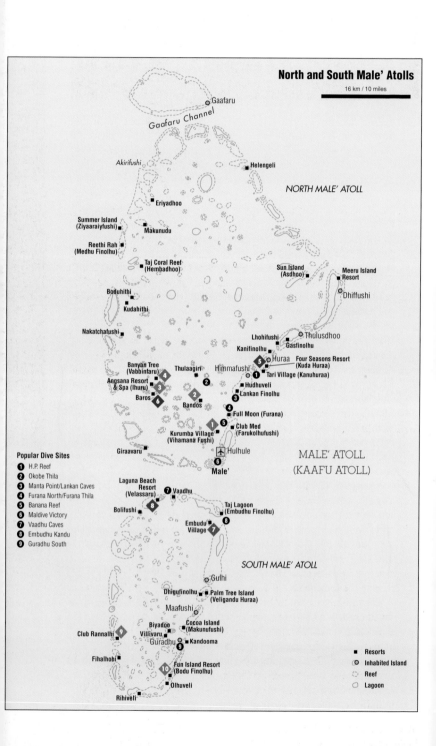

North and South Male' Atolls

16 km / 10 miles

Gaafaru

Gaafaru Channel

Akirifushi

Helengeli

NORTH MALE' ATOLL

Eriyadhoo

Summer Island
(Ziyaaraiyfushi)

Makunudu

Reethi Rah
(Medhu Finolhu)

Taj Coral Reef
(Hembadhoo)

Sun Island
(Asdhoo)

Meeru Island
Resort

Boduhithi

Dhiffushi

Kudahithi

Nakatchafushi

Lhohifushi   Thulusdhoo

Kanifinolhu   Gasfinolhu

Banyan Tree   Thulaagiri   Himmafushi   Huraa
(Vabbinfaru)

Four Seasons Resort
(Kuda Huraa)

Angsana Resort
& Spa (Ihuru)

Tari Village (Kanuhuraa)

Baros

Hudhuveli

Bandos   Lankan Finolhu

Full Moon (Furana)

Kurumba Village
(Vihamana Fushi)

Club Med
(Farukolhufushi)

Giraavaru

Hulhule

MALE' ATOLL
(KAAFU ATOLL)

Male'

Laguna Beach
Resort
(Velassaru)   Vaadhu

Bolifushi

Taj Lagoon
(Embudhu Finolhu)

Embudu
Village

SOUTH MALE' ATOLL

Gulhi

Dhigufinolhu   Palm Tree Island
(Veligandu Huraa)

Maafushi

Biyadoo   Cocoa Island
(Makunufushi)

Club Rannalhi   Villivaru

Guradhu   Kandooma

Fihalhohi

Fun Island Resort
(Bodu Finolhu)

Olhuveli

Rihiveli

Popular Dive Sites
1. H.P. Reef
2. Okobe Thila
3. Manta Point/Lankan Caves
4. Furana North/Furana Thila
5. Banana Reef
6. Maldive Victory
7. Vaadhu Caves
8. Embudhu Kandu
9. Guradhu South

■ Resorts
◎ Inhabited Island
◌ Reef
○ Lagoon

2. BANDOS *(see map, p22)*

No of rooms: 225; Distance from airport: 8 km (5 miles); Price range: $$$; Local agent: Bandos Male' Office, Iz'zaadgeen Magu, Male', tel: 32-5529, fax: 32-1026; Resort tel: 44-0088, fax: 44-3877, e-mail: sales@bandos.com.mv, web: www.bandos.com

Like Kurumba Village, Bandos first opened in 1972 and has undergone many changes since. Just 15 minutes from the airport by speedboat, it is one of the biggest resorts in the Maldives. This is a relatively large island though one side of it is quite rocky and has no beach. Nearby is the uninhabited island of Kuda Bandos, which is reserved for the locals as a public park on Fridays. During the rest of the week, Kuda Bandos is frequented by tourists from nearby resorts and is an ideal spot for excursions and picnics.

The resort is well laid out with wide sand walkways flanked by flowering plants and trees. You rarely have the feeling that there are 500 or more people around. A walk around the island is your only clue to its size. The reception complex, with its restaurants, shops and bar is the focal point on the island. Just behind the business centre is a convention centre for meetings and conferences. The air-conditioned rooms and suites are situated away from the activity centres in blocks of two or more, each with its own covered patio. The rooms are touted as "beachfront", although some are a good 50-metre (165-ft) walk from the beach. The interiors are spacious, with wide glass panels that allow a generous view of the surroundings.

The main restaurant – with open-air and air-conditioned sections – serves breakfast, lunch and dinner buffets for those on a full-board package, but independent travellers are welcome to have their meals here as well. The coffee house serves a good selection of Western and Asian fare. For dinner, there are more options with the Pasta Place and Harbour Grill.

Above: parasailing is offered by a few resorts
Right: typical accommodation at Bandos

The excellent house reef is ideal for snorkelling. There is a full range of water sports, including scuba diving, windsurfing, water-skiing, sailing and deep-sea fishing. Bandos is also one of the few resorts that offers parasailing.

The resort has its own shopping gallery with souvenir shops, a photo-shop for quick processing, a jewellery shop and a beauty salon. The sports complex is well-equipped, with a gymnasium, tennis and squash courts, a swimming pool and massage treatments. Daytime childcare is also available here.

Bandos has a fully staffed, 24-hour medical clinic and a four-person decompression chamber for diving accidents. The clinic can arrange for emergency transport by sea plane from your resort to the clinic.

Recently, Bandos has gained a reputation as a stop-over hotel for airline crews. In fact, it attracts a mixed clientele from Europe and Asia, from boisterous families to wide-eyed honeymooners. Good service and friendly staff contribute to the holiday feel of the island, as do little surprises like the crowing of a rooster at the start of each day.

3. ANGSANA RESORT AND SPA (IHURU)
(see map, p22)

No of rooms: 45; Distance from airport: 17 km (11 miles); Price range: $$$$; Book directly with the resort: tel: 44-3502, fax: 44-5933, e-mail: maldives@angsana.com, web: www.angsana.com

"I am Captain Matheen," says the young Maldivian greeting guests who board the small speed boat for the 30-minute cruise from the airport to the spa resort of Angsana. Maldivians are reserved, private people, but interaction with visitors has emboldened them to express themselves to strangers with quiet confidence. Captain Matheen concludes his carefully rehearsed speech of welcome by saying, "If there is an emergency, the crew will help you." His crew, two teenage lads, nod in agreement.

It is a warm welcome to one of the Maldives' newest resorts (opened in 2001). Although Angsana was previously famous as an ecologically aware resort going by its island name of Ihuru, its conversion by the Angsana group has transformed it into an entirely new resort. The commitment to the environment, however, remains, ensuring that the delicate surroundings of the island remain pristine and protected. Rubbish is disposed of carefully, and water is solar-heated.

The island of Ihuru (meaning 'old palm trees' in Dhivehi) spans an area of 2.5 hectares (6 acres) of lush greenery, with over 590 metres (645 yds) of the most beautiful palm-fringed beaches, with crystalline waters and kaleidoscopic reefs. A shallow lagoon with the reef just a few metres from the beach surrounds the island and is ideal for snorkelling and observing marine life.

Left: feeding a stingray in the shallows

Accommodation is in 45 beachfront villas, 10 of which have private Jacuzzis. The décor of each is a blend of tropical and contemporary styles, colourful and without clutter. An amusing feature is the placing of real fruit so it is framed by square holes in the walls. The bathrooms are open to the sky with the shower water spouting out of a granite column. All rooms are air-conditioned and have a fan, as well as a mini-bar, coffee- and tea-making facilities, a safe, direct-dial telephone, hairdryer and bathrobes. They have a veranda with dining and sitting area, and a Maldivian swing seat in the garden.

The special feature of the resort is the spa in the centre of the island, with eight treatment rooms providing a holistic, non-clinical experience that uses aromatherapy and massage to refresh and rejuvenate you. The spa staff are trained in Thailand at the Banyan Tree Academy, with which Angsana is associated.

Meals at Angsana are delicious affairs at the Riveli Restaurant and can also be taken on the beach, in your villa or as a picnic on a neighbouring sandbank. Angsana has all the usual water sports and diving facilities and can even arrange wedding ceremonies underwater, as well as on land.

4. BANYAN TREE (VABBINFARU)
(see map, p22)

No of rooms: 48; Distance from airport: 16 km (10 miles); Price range: $$$$$; Book directly with the resort: tel: 44-3147, fax: 44-3843, e-mail: maldives@banyantree.com, web: www.banyantree.com

If rest and relaxation are your top priorities, the 48-room Banyan Tree, which opened in 1995, will more than satisfy. Small and exclusive, it certainly disproves the adage that bigger is better. The setting is breathtaking: the island is one of the prettiest in North Male' Atoll, and like its neighbours Baros and Angsana, has one of the best house reefs around, thriving with an abundance of soft coral and colourful fish.

Above: chic styling at Angsana

The oversized villas, each with its own private garden, are capped with high-ceilinged spiral shaped roofs made of coir, and wooden shutters that can be thrown open for an unobstructed view of azure sea and sky. As in most Maldives resorts, you don't have to worry about security; many guests leave their doors open at night – lulled to sleep by the breeze and the lapping waves – and wake up to glorious vistas in the morning.

The rooms are very comfortable, with four-poster beds, huge bathrooms, private sun decks and works of art, but they are by no means over-the-top luxurious. There is a choice of garden or beach villas, the latter only a few steps away from the lagoon and costing more. In keeping with the natural ambience, there is no swimming pool, the calm clear waters of the lagoon more than adequately compensating for its absence.

It is clear that much thought has been given to the environment in the resort's design and operation. Much of the original vegetation was kept intact when the villas were erected and no coral was used as building material. Sewage is treated before it is disposed, and the use of plastics is discouraged; instead, biodegradable shampoo and conditioner are packed in reusable ceramic bottles.

With a generous staff-to-guest ratio of one to one, you are assured of attentive service. When it comes to dining, you can try a delicious four-course meal at the Ilaafathi Restaurant or a beach-side buffet at the outdoor Sangu Restaurant, and then retire to the Naiboli bar for after-dinner drinks.

In general, there is a lazy atmosphere at the resort. It is definitely not for those bent on organised activities and mass participation. A range of activities is available – snorkelling, scuba diving, sailing, water-skiing, fishing, windsurfing, canoeing and glass-bottom boat trips – but there are no gung-ho instructors pressing you to sign up. Stressed-out urbanites will find this and the resort spa, with its extensive range of body treatments, sheer bliss.

5. FOUR SEASONS RESORT (KUDA HURAA)
(see map, p22)

No of rooms: 106; Distance from airport: 12 km (7 miles); Price range: $$$$$; Book directly with the resort: tel: 44-4888, fax: 44-1188, e-mail: info@kudahuraa.com, web: www.fourseasons.com

In 1998, the ritzy Four Seasons group took over the former Kuda Huraa Reef, transforming an already top-class resort into something even better, if such a thing were possible. And the Four Seasons does pull it off – well, almost. Picture if you will 68 thatched beach bungalows – some with private plunge pools, others with outdoor garden bathrooms – on a narrow island fringed by sugar-white beaches on either side. Another 34 villas on stilts are perched above the water at one end of the island. Featuring huge bathrooms with glass picture windows opening out to vistas of shimmering water, it is not surprising that the water villas are a huge hit with honeymooners. You could order room service and not see the outside of your villa for an entire week if you chose to.

The rest of the 5-hectare (12-acre) resort manages to keep up with the standards set by the accommodation. The swimming pool, which seems to merge seamlessly into the surrounding sea, is one of the largest in the islands. You can sip cocktails on the Poolside Terrace or in the Nautilus Lounge and then stroll to one of the three restaurants for meals. The Café Huraa serves buffets for breakfast, lunch and dinner, while the Baraabaru Restaurant concentrates on evening *a la carte*

dining, and the Reef Club offers Mediterranean cuisine. The range and quality of the food served at the restaurants are exquisite: you would be forgiven for thinking you were dining in a big city restaurant instead of a remote island where every last ingredient needs to be shipped in on a daily basis. After indulging your taste buds, a relaxing herbal massage at the spa might be just the thing to send you floating back to your room.

If you are a more active sort, there is parasailing, water-skiing, big-game fishing, a fully equipped dive centre and a gymnasium to keep you occupied. Every day a notice is put up at the recreation centre with the day's schedule and activity suggestions. The one thing, however, that the Four Seasons could not transform with its magic wand was the lagoon – there are precious few corals to be found here and it is so large that swimming from the beach to the reef edge is not really practical. To compensate for this, snorkelling trips are organised daily for guests.

Top Left: one of the spacious bathrooms at Banyan Tree
Left: a Banyan Tree beach villa. **Above:** beach and jetty at Four Seasons

6. BAROS *(see map, p22)*

*No of rooms: 77; Distance from airport: 16 km (10 miles); Price range $$;
Local agent: Universal Enterprises, 39 Orchid Magu, Male', tel: 32-3080,
fax: 32-2678; Resort tel: 44-1920, fax: 44-3497, e-mail: bhr@
dhivehinet.net.mv, web: www.unisurf.com*

There are so many repeat visitors at Baros it is often difficult to get a room
here. The loyalty of regular visitors has been won through the resort offer-
ing not only quality and value for money, but also a good choice of accom-
modation. This consists of 59 deluxe rooms, two suites, and 16 superb
over-water suites. The rooms have direct access to the beach, yet remain
secluded by the island's lush vegetation.

The rooms are like cosy cabins with roofs of palm thatch, wooden floors,
furnishings of rattan, fine fabrics, and state-of-the-art fittings exuding good
taste. The water suites, each with its own private sun deck, are built on solid
columns over the aquamarine waters of the island's lagoon. Each stands
alone, accessed by a boardwalk, and each has an entrance hall, a bedroom
decorated in natural tones, with a four-poster bed, and a bathroom with full-
length bath. Every guest room and suite has air-conditioning and fans; acces-
sories include tea- and coffee-making facilities, mini-bar, hairdryer, safe, and
direct-dial telephone. Room service is available around the clock.

Although Baros is small, it is distinguished by having four fine restaurants,
including the Lagoon Restaurant for gourmet dining, the open-sided Gar-
den Restaurant for set dinners and buffets and the Palm Garden for Asian and
Oriental dishes, as well as a coffee shop. The Captain's Bar has nautical
décor and a convivial atmosphere. At the centre of 10 major dive sites, the
island is also a favourite with divers and snorkellers.

This is a popular resort, yet it is an island where the pursuit of pleasure
is a leisurely affair and where privacy and peace are preserved.

Above: water suites in the clear lagoon of Baros

South Male' Atoll

7. EMBUDU VILLAGE *(see map, p22)*

No of rooms: 124; Distance from airport: 8 km (5 miles); Price range: $; Local agent: Kaimoo Travel and Hotel Services, H. Roanuge, Male', tel: 32-2212, fax: 31-8057; Resort tel: 44-4776, fax: 44-2673, e-mail: embvil@ dhivehinet.net.mv, web: www.embuduvillage.com.mv

With sand as the floor of the reception area and also of the long lounge leading to the restaurant, Embudu Village signals to its guests that it's a resort without frills. With new resorts going in for elaborate back-to-nature décor, this resort's simplicity is welcome for those on a limited holiday budget. It also has the advantage of being close enough to the airport for transfer to be done by *dhoni* (motorised launch), in about 40 minutes.

There is one restaurant, with sandstone tiles instead of sand for the floor, where all three meals of the day are tasty buffets. Guests have the option of staying on full board or on the all-inclusive (unlimited drinks included) full-board package.

The bar is in a separate pavilion and offers two kinds of draught beer as well as the usual drinks. Volley ball, badminton and table tennis are the sports activities and there is a popular dive centre. There is no swimming pool since the lagoon is perfect for swimming and snorkelling, and the house reef is only 20 metres (65 ft) from the beach.

The resort has 36 standard rooms in blocks. They have fans, mosquito nets and wooden louvred doors to encourage air flow. The 72 superior rooms are in long blocks and are air-conditioned with telephone, shower, hairdryer and fridge. The exterior appearance of the 16 over-water rooms is formidable since they resemble a terrace of cement and corrugated-iron-roof bungalows in blocks of four. However, inside they have floors of wood into which is set an illuminated glass panel for watching fish in the lagoon below. They also have television as well as a telephone, bathtub, fridge and safe.

Holiday is what Embudu Village is all about, and there is a happy atmosphere enjoyed by guests who are mostly German-speaking, with a few British and French visitors as well.

Right: shooting the breeze at the bar at Embudu Village

8. Laguna Beach Resort (Velassaru)
(see map, p22)

No of rooms: 129; Distance from airport: 12 km (7 miles); Price range: $$; Local agent: Universal Enterprises, 39 Orchid Magu, Male', tel: 32-2971, fax: 32-2678; Resort tel: 44-5906, fax: 44-3041, e-mail: lbr@dhivehinet.net.mv, web: www.unisurf.com

Heading south from Male', sailing past Villingili and across Vaadhu Channel, one arrives at Laguna Beach Resort. This good-looking resort, which opened in 1990, sits at the northwest tip of South Male' Atoll. This is a favourite among the locally owned Universal chain of resorts in terms of ambience and layout.

The reception area has a high ceiling and carries heavy Filipino accents in its design. Accommodation is in bungalows, each separated by thick shrub and trees for privacy, in double-storey blocks away from the main activity area or in 17 luxury over-water suites. All rooms are equipped with mini-bar, tea- and coffee-making facilities, safe, hairdryer, umbrellas, piped music and direct-dial telephones. The deluxe rooms are attractively furnished, with a split-level lounge area and bedroom. Housekeeping gets top marks here: on one visit, a leaking tap was repaired just minutes after it was reported.

Laguna, which attracts a mix of the well-heeled and young families, is blessed with a stretch of soft sandy beach all around the island. There is also a splendid lagoon with thick clusters of soft brown corals and schools of colourful damselfish. The expansive lagoon is also ideal for windsurfing and sailing. There is a comprehensive list of activities to keep you on your feet, including two swimming pools, and a hydro-pool to soothe tired muscles.

Like the other Universal-owned resorts, Laguna has a good range of restaurants – the main Summer Fields restaurant for guests booked on a half-board or full-board arrangement, a coffee shop, an Italian restaurant, a Chinese restaurant, and a barbecue terrace overlooking the sea.

9. CLUB RANNALHI *(see map, p22)*

No of rooms: 116; Distance from airport: 34 km (21 miles); Price range: $$; Local agent: Jetan Travel Services, STO Aifaanu Building, Male', tel: 32-3323, fax: 31-7993; Resort tel: 44-2688, fax: 44-2035, e-mail: reserve@rannalhi.com.mv, web: www.aitkenspence.com/hotels

Completely redesigned in 1996, Club Rannalhi is Sri Lankan-owned and managed and bears the hallmark of the Aitken Spence group, which operates some of the best hotels in Sri Lanka. The resort is on the southwestern edge of South Male' Atoll, about 50 minutes by speedboat from the airport.

The architecture of the resort's two-storey beach villas is striking and shows a colonial touch, softened by thatched roofs. There are 100 air-conditioned standard rooms, each with mini-bar, hairdryer and telephone. The 16 slightly more luxurious over-water rooms are arranged in pairs in eight bungalows linked to the island by narrow wooden walkways. The bungalows also have deep-pitched thatched roofs, and the rooms inside have televisions as well as the usual facilities.

There is only one restaurant, where meals are usually served as buffets; its theme nights are especially popular. Before Aitken Spence took over, Club Rannalhi was a Club Med-style resort, and it has maintained its reputation for fun – there are lots of organised activities, which make this a resort for the party crowd rather than the solitude seeker.

However, there is a great beach of soft white sand that completely encircles the island, so you will be able to find some space to yourself. The lagoon is ideal for swimming (so there's no pool) and a variety of water sports, being shallow and sandy-bottomed.

The list of recreation activities includes diving (provided by a PADI dive school), snorkelling, night diving, catamaran sailing, windsurfing, water-skiing, banana boat riding, canoeing, big game fishing, aerobics, football, volleyball, badminton and table tennis. There is also a disco, and there are occasional karaoke and cultural show nights.

Top Left: two waiters among the lush foliage of Laguna Beach
Left: carefree days. **Above:** Club Rannalhi's two-storey accommodation

10. FUN ISLAND RESORT (BODU FINOLHU)
(see map, p22)

No of rooms: 100; Distance from airport: 38 km (24 miles); Price range: $; Local agent: Villa Hotels, 3rd Floor, STO Trade Centre, Orchid Magu, Male', tel: 31-6161, fax: 31-4565; Resort tel: 44-4558, fax: 44-3958, e-mail: fun@dhivehinet.net.mv, web: www.villahotels-maldives.com

Bodu Finolhu, like many islands in South Male' Atoll, is long and narrow. Access to the resort is by a long wooden jetty.

Extensively renovated in 1992, Fun Island caters to a variety of nationalities – Europeans, Australians, Japanese and Tai-wanese. The resort seems pretty popular with family groups, judging from the number of families there during one stay. In fact, the atmosphere reminds one of a holiday camp in Europe, with laundry lines hanging outside the terraced blocks and children chasing one another down the beach. This is not your ideal getaway for peace and tranquillity. The island is tiny, measuring 30 by 800 metres (100 ft by half a mile), but if it gets crowded here, you can easily walk over to the two nearby uninhabited islands at low tide.

The accomodation is set in terraced blocks of two to four rooms. Though not luxurious, you will find all that you need – air-conditioning, telephones, mini-bars, and hot and cold showers. The furnishings are a bit garish though, with bright lime-green curtains and red plastic flowers on the wall. Aside from the main restaurant, there is also a 24-hour coffee house. The most pleasant part of the resort is the bar, which opens out onto a wooden patio overlooking the sea where you can enjoy the sunset with a cocktail in hand.

The resort offers the standard range of water-sports facilities for a fee. Courses are given in windsurfing and catamaran sailing. The Delphis diving centre here is well-established in the Maldives. For the many Japanese guests, there is a Japanese dive instructor available.

Ari Atoll

11. KURAMATHI TOURIST ISLAND *(see map, p34)*

Distance from airport: 70 km (43 miles); Local agent: Universal Enterprises, 39 Orchid Magu, Male', tel: 32-3080, fax: 32-0274, e-mail: village@kuramathi.com.mv, web: www.unisurf.com

Kuramathi Tourist Island is the only island in the Maldives that has three separate resorts, each one different in style. They are all under the same management, and guests can use any bar or *à la carte* restaurant and have the bill charged to their room, even if they are staying in another of the island's resorts. An air-conditioned mini-bus shuttles the 1½-km (1-mile) length of the island to take guests from one resort to another.

Although it is possible to fly in 15 minutes by seaplane from the airport, the 90-minute cruise by luxury launch is popular as it takes you straight from the airport jetty to Kuramathi's pier. Travel by seaplane involves a bus ride and a *dhoni* hop as well, adding to the journey time.

Kuramathi Village

No of rooms: 151; Price range: $ and $$ (all-inclusive); Resort tel: 45-0623, fax: 45-0556

The palatial reception lobby (complete with cyber-café and television lounge) serves as the welcome centre for guests staying at all the island's resorts.

Three styles of room make up the Village accommodation. There are 47 standard rooms, which are circular in shape, with fan, air-conditioning, shower and toilet, and a simple veranda, hidden among the jungly foliage. The 33 superior rooms are square in shape with thatched roof and wooden floor and woven reed interior walls. They have fan and air-conditioning, a dressing room and deck veranda, as well as bathroom and bedroom. The 71 deluxe rooms feature a four-poster bed and a walled garden bathroom open to the sky. Each has a fan as well as modern air-conditioning, and a deck veranda with steps to the beach.

The resort's Fung Bar, with a counter in the shape of a *dhoni*, is a lively night spot. As well as the main restaurant and coffee shop, there is an Indian restaurant, the Tandoor Mahal, for evening dining.

Like the other two resorts, Kuramathi Village has its own diving centre. It also has a fully-equipped medical centre with resident doctors and a six-

Top Left: buffet dining. **Left:** the name says it all
Above: the beach at Kuramathi

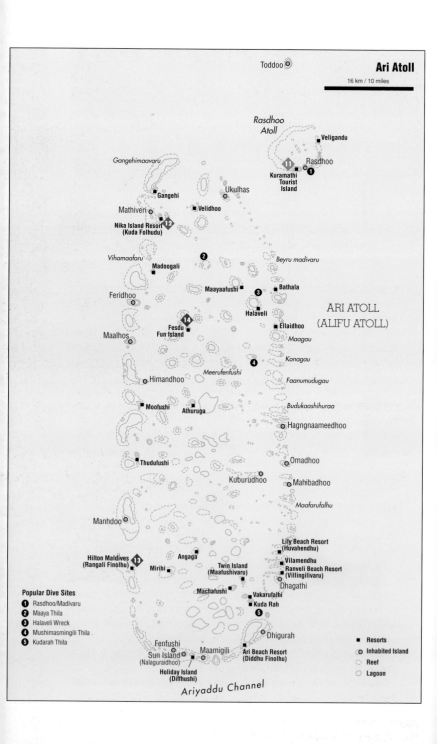

Ari Atoll

16 km / 10 miles

Toddoo

Rasdhoo Atoll

Veligandu

Gangehimaavaru

11 Rasdhoo
Kuramathi Tourist Island 1

Gangehi

Ukulhas

Mathiveri

Velidhoo

Nika Island Resort (Kuda Folhudu) 12

Vihamaafaru

Beyru madivaru

Madoogali

2

Maayaafushi

Bathala

Feridhoo

3

Halaveli

ARI ATOLL (ALIFU ATOLL)

Ellaidhoo

14 Fesdu Fun Island

Maagau

Maalhos

Konagau

4

Faanumudugau

Meerufenfushi

Himandhoo

Moofushi

Athuruga

Budukaashihuraa

Hagngnaameedhoo

Thudufushi

Omadhoo

Kuburudhoo

Mahibadhoo

Maafarufalhu

Manhdoo

Lily Beach Resort (Huvahendhu)

Angaga

Hilton Maldives (Rangali Finolhu) 13

Mirihi

Vilamendhu
Ranveli Beach Resort (Villingilivaru)

Twin Island (Maafushivaru)

Dhagathi

Machafushi

Vakarufalhi
Kuda Rah 5

Dhigurah

Popular Dive Sites
1 Rasdhoo/Madivaru
2 Maaya Thila
3 Halaveli Wreck
4 Mushimasmingili Thila
5 Kudarah Thila

Fenfushi

Maamigili

Sun Island (Nalaguraidhoo)

Ari Beach Resort (Diddhu Finolhu)

Holiday Island (Diffushi)

■ Resorts
◉ Inhabited Island
▢ Reef
○ Lagoon

Ariyaddu Channel

person decompression chamber for diving emergencies. An on-site shop specialises in marine items, and there is also a photo-processing laboratory.

Kuramathi Cottage Club
No of rooms: 50; Price range: $$ and $$$ (water villas); Resort tel: 45-0532, fax: 45-0642

Set halfway along the island, this is a compact resort with 30 standard rooms, each with a veranda and a bathroom with shower in a miniature open-air garden. Its 20 over-water suites have a dressing room, bedroom with four-poster bed, bathroom with tub and shower, and a balcony with steps into the lagoon. All rooms have a mini-bar, tea- and coffee-maker, hairdryer and telephone.

As well as its Malaafaiy Restaurant with *table d'hôte* and buffet meals, the resort has a coffee shop, the Palm Court Restaurant for daytime light meals and the delectable Siam Garden Thai restaurant for dinner. An unusual facility available to guests is the Marine Biological Station, where regular lectures are given on the underwater world.

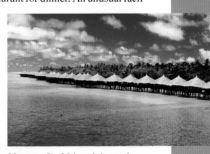

Kuramathi Blue Lagoon
No of rooms: 50; Price range: $$ and $$$ (all-inclusive); Resort tel: 45-0579, fax: 45-0531

Located at the tip of the island, this resort has been refurbished to give it an upmarket image, but it retains its natural charm and beauty. Its 30 beach bungalows have four-poster beds and bathtubs, and are tastefully decorated in warm tones. The 20 water suites are built over the lagoon. All rooms have a mini-bar, hairdryer, piped music and telephones. The main bar and restaurant are elegant, with an open-air deck for drinking sundowners. La Laguna Grill beside the beach serves meat and seafood, and there is a coffee shop, which also offers Asian cuisine. There is another bar at the resort's sports centre, which has a swimming pool, sauna, Jacuzzi, gymnasium, beauty salon and spa.

Above: the main bar on the island
Right: the over-water suites at the Cottage Club

12. NIKA ISLAND RESORT (KUDA FOLHUDU)
(see map, p34)

No of rooms: 28; Distance from airport: 74 km (46 miles); Price range $$$$$; Local agent: Nika Island Resort, 117 Majeedhee Magu, Male', tel: 32-5091, fax: 32-5097; Resort tel: 45-0516, fax: 45-0577, e-mail: nika@ dhivehinet.net.mv

Cruising southwest from Kuramathi one arrives at Nika Island Resort, on the northwestern tip of Ari Atoll. The seaplane transfer from Male' airport takes 30 minutes, followed by a short *dhoni* ride to the resort.

Named after a local tree, Nika was first leased by an Italian architect who built his dream home here in the 1980s. It was later converted into a small

hotel before being redesigned into its present incarnation. The island is luxuriantly green with coconut palms, screwpines and breadfruit trees. Soil was imported from Sri Lanka to plant vegetables and fruit trees, which accounts for the fresh salads and fruits served at mealtimes.

Total privacy is the top priority for the resort's 50-odd guests. For its high prices, you are housed in spacious bungalows, 70 sq meters (753 sq ft) in size. Well-camouflaged by thick foliage, each has its own little garden and a private stretch of beach for undisturbed sunbathing. Built of coral and wood, the bungalows are designed to resemble a shell, and the walls are subtly embellished with breadfruit leaf designs. High ceilings, fans and numerous windows keep the rooms cool. Luxury here is deliberately muted, and the rooms now look rather dated compared with newer resorts.

However, the buffet spread is superb, almost indulgent, with a wide selection of meat and fish dishes, pastas, salads, fruit and desserts. There is also a grill corner where you can have a steak done just the way you like it. A fine range of wines and champagne complement every meal.

13. HILTON MALDIVES (RANGALI FINOLHU)
(see map, p34)

No of rooms: 150; Distance from airport: 96 km (60 miles); Price range: $$$$; Book directly with the resort: tel: 45-0629, fax: 45-0619, e-mail: hilton@dhivehinet.net.mv, web: www.hilton.com

The Hilton has avoided the temptation to transplant a city hotel onto an island. This is a stylish and relaxing resort, but the five-star standards never slip.

The rooms are spread over two islands that are connected by a long, low bridge (a *dhoni* also shuttles between the two). On the main island are 100 beach villas with open-air bathrooms and private gardens, while on the smaller

Above: away from the beach on Nika Island

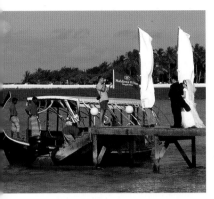

island are 50 water villas with direct access to the sea. Both types of villa feature timbered interiors that are beautifully designed using only natural materials and textiles.

For honeymooners and other solitary souls the smaller island is perfect. There is just one other building here, a small bar and café. The beach is good, not quite as good as the main island's, but only because the beach there is excellent: white, soft and stretching all the way around. The only downside to the small island is that there is no snorkelling here – you have to trek halfway over the bridge to a spot where the reef comes close.

The guests come from a wide variety of nationalities, ensuring a friendly and cosmopolitan atmosphere. An extensive list of excursions includes snorkelling 'safaris', with a visit to an uninhabited island for a barbecue. Windsurfing and deep-sea fishing are also available. The resort also operates a spa.

The main Atoll Restaurant serves a mix of Western and Asian dishes at each buffet. A more expensive option is the romantic Sunset Bar and Grill perched over water, with views of the lagoon and sunsets.

14. FESDU FUN ISLAND *(see map, p34)*

No of rooms: 60; Distance from airport: 72 km (45 miles); Price range $$ (all inclusive); Local agent: Universal Enterprises, 39 Orchid Magu, Male', tel: 32-3080, fax: 32-2678; Resort tel: 45-0541, fax: 45-0547, e-mail: fesdu@ kuramathi.com.mv, web: www.unisurf.com

Fesdu, with its circular shape, superb white sands fringed with coconut palms and translucent lagoon, is the archetypal tropical island. Its lush vegetation conceals attractive guest cottages with thatched, conical-shaped roofs, each one only a step away from the gorgeous beach.

The rooms at Fesdu are designed for the holiday escapist: no TV, no telephone, no room service, no mini-bar, no bathtub, just a shower with hot and cold water. They have a wooden-faced exterior, an interior of basket-weave panels and a large, tiled veranda bedecked with flowers.

The all-inclusive rate is extraordinarily generous, as it includes unlimited cocktails, mineral water, soft drinks, beer, spirits, liqueurs, house wine, tea and coffee, sandwiches, buffet breakfast, lunch and dinner, plus a sunset cruise, snorkelling equipment hire, table tennis and windsurfing (but no lessons). No wonder so many of its guests return as often as they can.

Above: wedding photos at the Hilton
Right: a secluded corner

Baa Atoll

15. SONEVA FUSHI RESORT & SPA (KUNFUNADHOO)
(see map below)

*No of rooms: 62; Distance from airport: 96 km (60 miles); Price range:
$$$$$; Book directly with resort: tel: 23-0304, fax: 23-0335; e-mail:
sonresa@soneva.com.mv, web: www.six-senses.com*

This resort has attracted a lot of attention, probably because of the charm and
genius of its creators, Sonu and Eva Shivdasani. It merges enchantingly into
the wilderness of Kunfunadhoo, at 1,400 metres (1 mile) long and 400 metres
(¼ mile) wide, one of the largest islands, 30 minutes by seaplane from the
airport. Its villas of timber combine the utmost luxury with whimsical extras,
like shoescrapers designed as hedgehogs and bamboo-ladder towel racks.

There are several different room designs. The most modestly priced are
the 25 beachfront Rehendi rooms with open-air private garden bathroom with
bathtub and shower. The 12 Crusoe villas are beachfront duplexes with upstairs
bedroom and downstairs garden bathroom, while three deluxe versions have
the same layout but with a free-standing bathtub and separate shower.

In the 14 Soneva Fushi villas beside the beach there is a spacious bedroom
and a huge open-air bathroom. There are also five Soneva Fushi Villa suites
of vast rooms, an owner's villa and a huge presidential villa.

All rooms have the amenities associated with luxury properties, including air-conditioning and fans. The choice of building materials was dic-
tated by a desire for sustainable
development, thus materials such
as pine, recycled telegraph poles
and railway sleepers, palm wood,
bamboo and plantation (not rain
forest) teak have been used. Interior items have been fashioned
from waste products like water
hyacinth (the reeds that clog rivers)
and papier mâché (old newspapers
covered by rice paper). One guest
liked his room contents so much,
he bought all the furniture and had
it shipped to his home in Germany.

The resort has a fitness and health
spa and a diving school. There are
two restaurants and bars on opposite sides of the island. Each villa
has bicycles on which guests can
explore the sand trails of the island.

Map legend:
- ■ Resorts
- ◉ Inhabited Island
- ⬡ Reef
- ○ Lagoon

Baa Atoll

10 km / 8 miles

Map labels: Fenfushifaru, Vilingili, Vadhoo, Maammagaafaru, Moresby Channel, Bathalaa, Dhigufaru, Kashidhoo, Boyfuri, Kudarikilu, Keydhoo, Kamadhoo, Kendhoo, Reethi Beach Resort (Fonimagoodhoo) 17, Fahris, Finurus, Magoodhoo, Club Valtur, Royal Island (Horubadhoo) 16, Daravandhoo, Hibalhidhoo, Eydhafushi 15, Soneva Fushi Resort & Spa (Kunfunadhoo), Maadhoo, Vilingili, Coco Palm Resort & Spa (Dhunikolhu) 18, Thuladhoo, Kudadhoo, Hithadhoo, Kanifushi, Bodufinolhu, Olhugiri, Maduwari

In this natural haven, there are even Internet terminals tucked away in the library, itself hidden by foliage, and an underground wine cellar with some great wines, including some from Sonu and Eva's own collection.

Overall, though, it's the designer rusticity of Soneva Fushi that makes a holiday here such a unique experience.

16. ROYAL ISLAND (HORUBADHOO)
(see map, p38)

No of rooms: 150; Distance from airport: 110 km (68 miles); Price range: $$; Local agent: Villa Hotels, 3rd Floor, STO Trade Centre, Orchid Magu, Male', tel: 31-6161, fax: 31-4565; Resort tel: 23-0088, fax: 23-0099, e-mail: info@royal-island.com.mv, web: www.villahotels.com

This is the newest resort in Baa Atoll, opened in 2001. It is an island with a history since it has many huge banyan trees, possibly associated with a Buddhist past, as well as an ancient public bath. Appropriately, the resort's modern Royal Araamu Spa is located beside the ancient spa; it provides a variety of treatments including aromatherapy, reflexology, herbal scrubs, local massages, Indian ayurveda treatments, pedicure, manicure and facials. There are also Jacuzzis, a steam bath and a dry sauna.

The vegetation of the island has been carefully preserved, while the most modern buildings (for the power, water and waste-disposal plants, and for staff accommodation) have been built out of sight behind the guest rooms. The kitchen (you can take a guided tour) is possibly the finest in the islands. There is also a medical centre with resident doctor and a ward for patients.

The guest accommodation consists of 148 individual beachfront cottages, built of wood and carefully concealed by vegetation. The hallmark of the operators, Villa Hotels, is their modern city-hotel facilities, and Royal Island is no exception.

Above: stylish interior, Soneva Fushi
Right: asleep in paradise

Each villa has air-conditioning and fan, bathtub, open-air shower, hairdryer, bidet, direct-dial telephone, satellite television, in-house movies, safe, Internet and e-mail facilities, and a tea- and coffee-maker. There are also two presidential suites with private sun deck and their own bar, butler service, kitchen and dining room.

The main restaurant is called the Maakana and features a large lobster pond. All three meals here are served as buffets, but fine dining is available at the Raabondhi Restaurant and Bar. Other bars include one beside the pool, the 24-hour Boli Bar and the Chameleon Fun Pub with its pool table and karaoke. There is also a diving centre, and a water-sports outlet offering jet-skiing and kite-surfing.

17. REETHI BEACH RESORT (FONIMAGOODHOO)
(see map, p38)

No of rooms: 100; Distance from airport: 104 km (65 miles); Price range: $; Local agent: Magic Kingdom Resorts, Ma. Raarohige, Joashi Higun, Male', tel: 32-3758, fax: 32-8842; Resort tel: 23-2626, fax: 23-2727, e-mail: info@reethibeach.com.mv

Since it opened in 1998, this resort has already attracted a high percentage of repeat visitors, lured back perhaps by the informal, happy mood that prevails here. This is especially true at the SeaXplorer diving centre (www.sea-explorer.net), which organises superb diving opportunities, and at the water-sports school (www.h2o-world.net) where instruction is given in many water sports, including kite-surfing.

In the main restaurant, meals are served as buffets and there is also a speciality restaurant serving Chinese and Maldivian food. The Reethi Grill features seafood, including lobster, and mixed-grill nights. The main Rasgefaanu bar has an extended deck covered by palms and an adjacent room with snooker, table tennis and darts. There is also an *a la carte* coffee shop, a pool bar and a sunset bar on the beach.

There are 30 water villas, built in pairs and sharing a hall that has a floor

Above: swaying palms
Left: swing seat, Reethi Beach

open to the sea. In addition there are 36 deluxe and 34 standard beachfront rooms furnished in dark wood. All rooms have air-conditioning, hairdryer, mini-bar, direct-dial telephones and television. The island suits those on a modest budget and is very popular, often being fully booked.

18. COCO PALM RESORT AND SPA (DHUNIKOLHU)
(see map, p38)

No of rooms: 98; Distance from airport: 124 km (77 miles); Price range: $$$$ (suites: $$$$$); Local agent: Sunland Hotels, 04-01 STO Trade Centre, Orchid Magu, PO Box 20145, Male', tel: 32-4658, fax: 32-5543, e-mail: sunland@dhivehinet.net.mv; Resort tel: 23-0011, fax: 23-0022, e-mail: cocopalm@dhivehinet.net.mv, web: www.cocopalm.com.mv

Life is low key at the beautiful Coco Palm Resort, in keeping with the management's philosophy of leaving guests alone to do what they wish. For a holiday of escapism in serene surroundings, Coco Palm is the answer. Guests can spend each day in total leisure, or snorkel and dive off the pure white-sand beaches, cruise the atoll in a wooden 18-metre (59-ft) yacht or luxuriate at the Mandara spa, where treatments draw on the ancient health traditions of Asia.

This half-moon of an island, approximately 700 metres (½ mile) by 300 metres (328 yds) at its widest, is isolated at the southwest tip of Baa Atoll,

yet only 30 minutes by seaplane from the airport. Although there are 84 beachfront villas, they cannot be seen from the sea as the vegetation has been preserved so that the island looks as idyllic as it did before the resort was built.

All the villas, including the 12 lagoon villas, are the same size – 87 sq metres (936 sq ft). They have either kingsize or four-poster beds and the usual amenities of air-conditioning and fan, direct-dial telephone, safe, mini-bar, tea- and coffee-maker and hairdryer. The interior design indicates genteel good taste, with Indonesian antiques blending with

contemporary rattan fittings. The beach villas have an open-air garden bathroom with shower, and the deluxe versions have a sunken bath as well.

The lagoon villas, grouped around a horseshoe-shaped network of wooden jetties, have the ultimate luxury of a private freshwater splash pool set into the wooden deck over the lagoon. The two lagoon palace suites, at 154 sq metres (1,657 sq ft) in area, have splash pools large enough to swim in.

For those who really want to get away from it all, Coco Palm arranges a two-day champagne cruise for two on its yacht, as well as private picnics on an uninhabited island. Couples can also try being a castaway on a desert island – staff will serve a barbecue at night before marooning you to sleep in a hut under the stars. That, surely, is the escapist's ultimate fantasy.

Above: sun deck of a lagoon villa at Coco Palm

Excursions

EXCURSION 1. MALE' *(see map below)*

Ten minutes by boat from Male' International Airport lies the capital island
of Male' (pronounced Mah-ley). This is the geographical centre of the Maldives, the focal point of all trade and commerce, and the site for all gov-
ernmental and administrative affairs.

Male' is tiny for a capital city. An island of only 1.8 sq km (0.7 sq mile),
including reclaimed land to the south and west, Male' houses some 70,000
people, about 25 percent of the Maldives' total population. Add to this the
hundreds of people who visit from the outer islands to stay a few days and
students who board here, and the population density is very high. However,
except when the schools empty out, the streets never seem very crowded,
although the houses are built very close together.

The construction of new buildings goes on everywhere in this rapidly
expanding city. Although you can walk from one end to the other in 20 minutes, Male' has an excessively high number of cars, the result of new affluence brought about by development. There are now traffic lights in the city,
and even parking regulations, but since the roads are tiled like pedestrian
walkways, visitors should keep in mind that they are real roads and take
care when crossing – cars have right of way, except at pedestrian crossings.

While the average tourist is not likely to stay a night in Male', most
resorts organise half-day trips to the capital for sightseeing and shopping.
Nearby resorts in North and South Male' atolls offer as many as five excur-

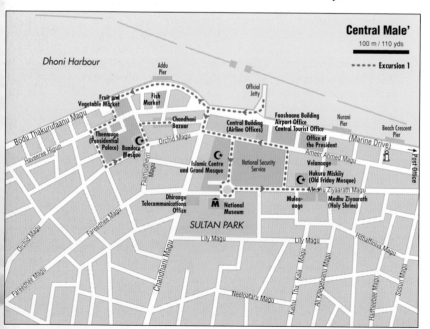

sions to Male' a week. Resorts normally avoid scheduling tours to the capital on Fridays, an official weekend day in this Islamic country, as most places of interest and offices are closed. However most shops open again in the evening, and the Botanical Gardens in Sultan Park is open on Fridays *only*. Rates for resort-organised excursions vary from US$20 to US$80, depending on the distance, the size of the tour group and whether lunch is provided. For resorts in the further-flung Ari and Baa atolls, transfers to Male' can be costly and troublesome. If time allows, some try to include a trip to Male' for their guests on the day of departure.

If you do decide to spend a night or two on Male', possibly to shop around for resort packages among the city's travel agents or to see a little of urban Maldivian life, accommodation is available at a few hotels and guesthouses. These are listed in the *Practical Information* section at the end of this book *(see pages 87–8)*. In fact, a stay in Male' is the best way to interact with ordinary Maldivians going about their daily business. As a resort guest, the only local people you will meet are the hotel staff.

A Tour of the City

Most resort *dhonis* arrive at the inner harbour on the north side of Male', near the **Official Jetty**, which is strictly reserved for the President and high-ranking officials. Upon arrival you are likely to be greeted by polite freelance tour guides. They can be helpful in identifying places of interest for you, but depend for their income on you buying souvenirs from their shops.

Having stepped off the *dhoni*, you will find yourself on what was once known as Marine Drive. This street is now known as **Bodu Thakurufaanu Magu**, commemorating the country's national hero, Bodu (Great) Thakurufaan, who led the uprising against the Portuguese occupation in the 16th century. This is the waterfront road and it circles the whole island. Don't worry too

much about road names, however; street signs are not easy to find and are usually written in the local script, *Thaana*, which is of little help to the visitor. It is useful, though, to know that *magu* means a wide street, *goalhi* is a narrow alley and *higun* is a longer lane. It is easy to get lost in the maze of narrow streets, but rest assured that you won't be lost for long, given the size of the island. Fortunately, the few places of interest that you are likely to visit are located near each other.

Above: children chatting on the sea wall
Right: Bodu Thakurufaanu Magu

In front of the jetty, across the green spread of **Jumhooree Maidan**, or **Republic Park**, is the **Islamic Centre**, whose main feature is the **Grand Mosque** with its golden dome, which can be seen from the sea as you approach Male' from the north. The Islamic Centre has a library, a conference hall and classrooms for religious studies. Opened in 1984, its prominence is a reflection of the important role that Islam plays in the lives of Maldivians.

The stunning Grand Mosque (open daily 9am–5pm, except during prayer times) can accommodate up to 5,000 worshippers. Its interior is adorned with woodcarvings and Arabic calligraphy, all painstakingly produced by Maldivian craftsmen. On Fridays, men dressed in their best congregate for the weekly prayers *(hukuru namaad)*, while women pray at home or in separate mosques. Bear in mind that this is a place of worship and therefore does not welcome hordes of gawking tourists. Should you wish to visit the mosque, it is advisable to be accompanied by a Maldivian. Visitors are requested to dress appropriately (footwear should be removed) and to observe strict silence.

The National Museum

As you come out of the mosque, you will find yourself on a little shady path called Iburaahimee Magu. The white wall facing you is part of the headquarters of the National Security Service. Just a few metres to the right you will see a roundabout and the main road of Medhu Ziyaarath Magu. Just across the road stands **Sultan Park**, which was once part of the sultan's palace, and is now a quiet retreat from the hustle and bustle of Male'. Much of the original palace was destroyed when the Sultanate was abolished, and the one remaining three-storey building was converted into the **National Museum** (open daily except Fridays and public holidays, 9am–noon and 3–6pm).

On display in the museum are an extensive collection of clothes and ornaments used by past sultans and sultanas, handwritten *Quran* scriptures and interesting pre-Islamic stone statues unearthed from the islands. Among these is the head of a Buddha image found on the island of Toddoo. Another precious artefact is a 13th-century wooden panel inscribed with ancient scriptures. One particularly intriguing exhibit is the motorbike situated near the entrance. This was used by one of the defending guards during the attempted coup in 1988 and bears holes from bullets fired at him by the mercenaries. A few of the museum caretakers speak English and will answer your questions.

On the same road as the museum, just two minutes' walk to the east, is the **Mulee-aage**, formerly the Presidential Palace, with its ornate gates and security posts. The colonial-style building housed the office of the president while the new Presidential Offices were being built on the waterfront. The building was designed by Ceylonese architects and was commissioned by Sultan Muhammed Shamsuddeen III for his son in 1906. In May 1936, due to a political rift, the Sultan and his son were banished to the island of Fua Mulaku and the palace was consequently declared government property. It was used

Above: pre-Islamic sculptures in the National Museum
Top Right: workers loading cement at Male' harbour. **Right:** the Friday Mosque

for government offices from 1942 to 1953, when it became the President's official residence. In 1986, the president moved to the current Presidential Palace (Theemuge) on Orchid Magu. Adjoining the Mulee-aage is the **Medhu Ziyaarath**, a shrine built over the grave of Abu'al Barakath, the man responsible for bringing Islam to the Maldives.

Opposite the Mulee-aage is the oldest and most beautiful mosque in Male', the old **Friday Mosque**, or **Hukuru Miskiiy**, built in 1656. The outside walls of the mosque are built with coral stones snugly fitted together without masonry, and the interior has old woodcarvings inscribed with Arabic writings which have been carefully preserved. In the garden within its compound are four wells for ritual ablutions and a sundial which was formerly used to calculate daily prayer times. Entry to the mosque is not permitted unless you have a special permit from an institution which is the authority for Islamic affairs.

In the cemetery next to the Friday Mosque stand a number of elaborate tombstones erected in memory of past heroes such as Sultan Ibrahim Iskandar I. Tombstones with pointed tops indicate that the grave belongs to a man, while the rounded stones mark that of a woman. Outside the mosque stands an imposing white minaret. Built a year after the mosque was erected, it was used for the call to prayer in earlier times.

The Bustling Markets

A block after turning left at the Friday Mosque, you find yourself on **Ameer Ahmed Magu**, where most of the government offices are located. Hundreds of bicycles are usually parked along here – it is quite a novel sight in the afternoons when workers in their white shirts and ties take off *en masse* on their bicycles. Should you require any tourist information, the Maldives Tourist Promotion Board is on the fourth floor of the Bank of Maldives

building, a couple of blocks east on the waterfront. The post office is further along to the east, beside the Nasandhura Palace Hotel.

Turning left again and walking down Ameer Ahmed Magu, you pass the headquarters of the **National Security Service**, which you caught a glimpse of earlier. Forget about taking pictures of the rifle-toting uniformed guard outside – it is prohibited.

Going past the Islamic Centre again and turning right towards the waterfront, you find yourself once more on Bodu Thakurufaanu Magu (Marine Drive). The area that you see to the left is the market and goods receiving area – the busiest section of the city. Here there is a perpetual confusion of people and activities at any hour of the day as Male' is a big distribution centre for the other islands.

If you are in Male' in the late afternoon, you may chance upon the highlight of the day – the return of the fishing boats. *Dhonis* spilling over with tuna, skipjack and bonito pull into the harbour just in front of the **Fish Market** for the crew to unload their catch of the day. The market is dominated by men, and of course, camera-toting tourists. This is not a place for the queasy as the air is always filled with the acrid smell of fresh blood and sweat.

Two blocks further down is the local market area. The sheltered area in front is where firewood from the outer islands is brought in and traded. At the back is the covered produce market, with its locally grown fruit, vegetables and spices. Leaves used for chewing betelnut are hugely popular. Coconuts are abundant, and a few *rufiyaa* will buy you some fresh coconut juice. The vendor will hack open the top of a green coconut, insert a straw and voila!

Coming out of the market you will find the imposing white walls surrounding **Theemuge**, the new **Presidential Palace**. Walk around the block for a glimpse of the blue and white palace through the front gates. Now you are on **Orchid Magu**, ready to head for the main shopping area known as **Chandhani Bazaar** (*see page 69*).

EXCURSION 2. FISHING VILLAGES
(see maps, pages 22, 34 and 38)

Confined to the often limited space of a resort island, you may begin to feel restless and ready to experience a bit of local colour. In which case, an island-hopping excursion is the perfect thing to do. As well as the regular shopping trips to Male', the capital *(see pages 42–6)*, many resorts also offer a half-day trip by *dhoni* to a nearby fishing village, followed by a visit to another resort for a spot of snorkelling or a picnic.

In the atolls that don't have resorts, the fishing villages, classified as 'inhabited islands', are strictly out of bounds to visitors. You need a special permit from the Ministry of Atolls Administration to visit such islands. However, many resorts have an arrangement for their guests to visit nearby fishing islands on organised excursions. These excursions, which cost US$15 or more per person, are the closest you'll get to seeing authentic village life on the islands.

Several inhabited islands open to visitors are found in North and South Male' and Ari atolls, where most of the resorts are located. To give you an idea, resorts in North Male' Atoll normally organise visits to the popular fishing villages at **Himmafushi** and **Huraa** islands. If you are staying at one of the resorts in South Male' Atoll, one of the most visited islands nearby is **Gulhi**, once famous for its boat-builders, who are now markedly absent. Other popular destinations include **Guradhu** and **Dhiffushi** islands.

For those staying in Ari Atoll, there are many lovely fishing villages to discover, among them **Toddoo**, where the ruins of an ancient Buddhist temple have been found. Toddoo is also famous for its sweet watermelons, which the locals relish during the fasting months. **Rasdhoo**, **Feridhoo**, **Dhagathi** and **Dhigurah** are other islands frequented by resort excursions in this atoll. In Baa Atoll, it is possible to visit the developed island of **Eydhafushi**, a thriving town with electricity and a new harbour, 116 km (72 miles) north of Male', and close to the resort island of Soneva Fushi.

While urbanisation is fast catching up in Male', and bringing with it the corresponding social problems, some of the more remote inhabited islands have remained largely unchanged. Over the years, however, many of the fishing villages that play host to the tourist excursions have seen changes brought about by tourism. One obvious consequence is the long row of small tourist shops that greet visitors as they step off the *dhoni*. Nevertheless, the islands still offer an interesting insight into the traditional Maldivian lifestyle.

As the island villages are generally similar in character, the following description of a visit to Dhagathi gives an idea of what to expect.

Top Left: Theemuge, the new Presidential Palace. **Left:** tuna fishing
Above: village woman polishing coral for necklaces

A Visit to Dhagathi

The island of Dhagathi – home to around 500 people – is on the southeast rim of Ari Atoll. As you approach the island in a *dhoni*, you will see an old *nika* tree rising high above the tops of the palm trees. Your guide may explain that this tree is of particular importance to the islanders, serving as a navigational guide for boats returning home, especially at night.

The water around Dhagathi is surprisingly clear and the white sandy beach remarkably clean. When you arrive at the jetty a group of excited children often run up to the boat to greet the new arrivals. As you disembark, you can see right across the island to the ocean on the other side.

A couple of tourist shops selling souvenirs line the road leading up from the beach. Among them is a provision shop, a cramped little store that provides basic household essentials for the villagers.

Beyond, the main coral-paved road runs through the island. From this, side-roads branch out leading to a maze of narrow paths and houses. The simple houses are made of coral and wood, with thatched roofs of native *cadjan* – dried palm leaves threaded together with coir rope. Outside many of the houses are *joali*, hammock-like chairs in which one can relax and chat with passing neighbours, or while away the afternoon. A coral wall surrounding the compound provides a measure of privacy, enclosing a garden and an open-air bathroom with *cadjan* walls.

The interiors of the houses are simply furnished. Perhaps the most comfortable place for a siesta is the *undhoali* outside, a wooden bed strung up by coir rope under the shade of a big tree.

On the beach itself, you will often find women tending to racks of salted fish drying under the

Above: a family outside their house
Left: weaving a grass mat

blazing sun. While the men go out fishing, the women tend to their homes and children. In some villages, you may see women involved in activities such as coir-making and mat-weaving, for use in their own homes.

In many fishing villages, especially those around Male', you will notice a scarcity of men. Many have abandoned fishing and taken up jobs in the capital or the resorts, leaving their families behind in the villages. Some only return after a year to spend a month with their families before returning to their jobs. Fortunately, there is a strong communal feeling among the villagers and close ties between families. The menfolk's prolonged absences also explain the many half-built houses you see throughout the village. The average Maldivian takes about three years to build his house, simply because he is never around to complete it.

In an open area on Dhagathi, a big wooden shed serves as the village kindergarten, where lessons are conducted with blackboard and chalk in the *Dhivehi* language. Here, where television and computer games have yet to invade, children content themselves with playing games on the beach and swimming in the lagoons. By the age of 10, most boys will have mastered three very important basic skills: sailing, fishing and swimming.

Boat Builders

On the beach on the other side of the island is the boat-making area. Similar in form to that of the Arabian dhow, the hull of the *dhoni* is made of coconut trunks and then reinforced with imported timber. Without a blueprint, the art of *dhoni*-making has been passed down through the generations by practice and word of mouth.

It takes a team of four to five carpenters, called *kissaru vadin*, about 40 days to build a standard 10-metre (33-ft) *dhoni*. When the boat is completed, fish oil is spread over the hull to ensure a smooth and safe journey and protect it from wood rot. Practically every family in the fishing villages owns a *dhoni* of some size. The basic form of the *dhoni* has seen few changes; many still maintain their triangular cotton sails.

Back in the village you may be offered the chance to share a Maldivian tea, generally consisting of *gula* (fish balls), *theluli bambukeo* (fried breadfruit), *keyku* (fluffy cake) and *kirusa* (tea with milk and sugar). As you eat, members of the family will sit around, laughing and chatting. If you're lucky, someone will offer you a puff on a *gudu-guda* or hubble-bubble (so named from the sound produced by the bubbles in the water pipe's glass container). Inhale deeply to taste the local blend, a mixture of imported tobacco and syrup drawn from the sap of the coconut tree. With a couple of deep drags you'll find yourself leaving the island on a particularly high note.

Right: the traditional craft of *dhoni* making

Diving

The Maldives is one of those rare destinations that offer excellent diving opportunities for all levels, from novice to expert. Instruction is available to meet every need, from resort courses for those taking the plunge for the first time to advanced and speciality courses for experienced divers. For novices, there are flat fields of soft corals, gentle slopes and dense aggregations of fish. For experienced divers, there are opportunities for drift diving and night diving, and there are plenty of steep walls, pinnacles and caverns to explore. There is also the chance to do a wreck dive. And for the group in between, there is an endless variety of reefs just waiting to be explored.

All the resorts operate diving schools and many have a 'house reef' you can access from the beach. If you want to enjoy the convenience of beach diving, check beforehand that the resort you have chosen has an accessible house reef. Otherwise, you would have to take a boat out to get to the reefs. For those who wish to venture further afield, live-aboard yacht-*dhonis* run dive safaris to some of the more remote reefs.

Good diving is found everywhere, although the Maldives and many other coral reefs of the world experienced a period of severe coral bleaching in the early part of 1998. Coral bleaching occurs when corals are exposed to prolonged high sea temperatures, which kills the small algae living in the coral tissues and turns entire reefs white. Although it is a regular occurrence associated with El Niño weather patterns, the long-term effect on the reefs is not clearly understood. What is certain though is that within a year, new coral formation usually occurs, mostly from fast-growing branching and table corals. Despite the rise in water temperatures, soft corals, sea fans and sponges were mostly unaffected in 1998, and on the deeper reefs and in the channels where there is more water movement, the effect of coral bleaching is less obvious.

In 1995, the government of the Maldives set aside 15 protected marine areas within the major tourist zones as part of a long-term strategy to conserve the marine environment. A further step forward was made in September 1998, when shark fishing was officially banned in the tourist atolls. Dynamite fishing is unknown in the region, and spear-fishing was outlawed in the mid-70s.

If you have never dived before and are in good health, short resort courses are available, as are various certification, speciality and advanced courses. Bring your diving certification card (C-card) and your log book, as reputable dive operators will ask to see them. You may be asked to do a checkout dive, or at least an easy initial dive so that the divemaster can see how comfortable you are in the water.

Left: a shimmering school of fish
Right: preparing for a dive

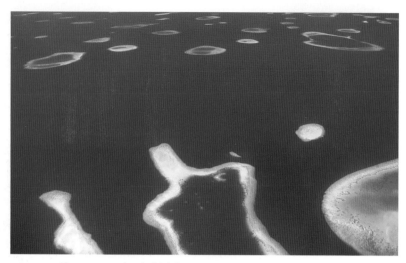

If you are staying in Male' you can arrange a day trip to dive with one of the nearby resorts or you can contact one of the Male'-based dive operators, such as Sea Explorers Dive School (tel: 31-6172, fax: 31-6783, email: seaexplo@dhivehinet.net.mv).

Maldivian Reefs

The Maldives, a double strand of atolls covering over 90,000 sq km (34,750 sq miles) of the Indian Ocean, forms the central part of the volcanic Laccadives-Chagos Ridge. Its 26 geographical atolls include Huvadhoo, one of the largest atolls in the world.

Atolls are generally believed to form when ancient volcanoes surrounded by fringing reefs subside into the ocean. As the volcanic landmass slowly sinks, the coral reef around the edges continues to build up. This process continues until the volcano is completely submerged and only the built-up coral ring, or atoll, remains. Natural breaks in the reef form the passes now used by boats to move in and out of the atolls. Over time, sand and coral debris build up on the reef and form low-lying islands. The process of atoll formation takes millions of years and was first recognised by Charles Darwin in the 1830s. His theory of atoll formation has been substantiated by a number of ocean-drilling and test-bore samples taken during the past 50 years.

The calm, clear, warm waters in the lagoons provide favourable conditions for the formation of large areas of branching and reef-building corals that are home to many of the 700 or so species of fish found here. If you wish to identify the fish, look for a fish identification book called *Photo Guide to Fishes of the Maldives*, by Rudie H. Kuiter, or a series of informative books by Charles Anderson.

Above: reefs in North Male' Atoll
Left: checking equipment on a dive *dhoni*

diving

There are many types of coral reef formations and they are all given names in the local language, *Dhivehi*. A *faru* is a reef partially exposed at low tide and a *falhu* is often a reef encircling a lagoon, sometimes with one or more islands inside. Inside the atolls are many ring-shaped coral reefs called *faros*. These formations are not unique to the Maldives, but the fact they occur here with such frequency is. A *giri* is the name for a small patch of coral close to the surface. Most resorts have their own *bodu giri* (big reef) and *kuda giri* (small reef) nearby, which are accessible to both divers and snorkelers. A *thila* is a coral reef usually a few metres below the surface. Many dive sites, such as Nassimo Thila, Miyaru Thila and Okobe Thila have names that indicate the presence of such a reef formation.

The channels cutting through the outer reefs of the atolls are called *kandus*. These can range in depth from 15 to 40 metres (50 to 130 ft), while the channels separating the atolls can be more than 300 metres (1,000 ft) deep. At the entrance of the *kandus* divers can find caves and overhangs with soft corals, sponges and sea fans and a multitude of pelagics (fish that inhabit the open sea), including trevally, shark and barracuda. Currents can be very strong in the channels so drift diving is the usual method here, giving divers greater opportunity to see more reef and marine life than could otherwise be found.

The outer walls of the atolls drop off sharply to much greater depths, where the surrounding waters can be anywhere between 1,000 and 3,000 metres (3,300–10,000 ft) deep. There are a few vertical walls, and although many outer reefs have steep slopes, there are some places where the drop-off is gradual.

Inside the atolls, depth is around 30 metres (100 ft), and diving is generally more protected. Visibility inside the atolls can vary but it is generally quite good. Each island is fringed by its own 'house reef', which provides opportunities for easy beach diving at many of the resort islands.

When to Dive

The very best time to dive is between January and April, when the seas are calm, the skies are sunny and the water is at its clearest, with visibility well over 30 metres (100 ft). Beginning in late August and continuing through October, whales are seen in the channel at the southern tip of Ari Atoll. But if you want to see manta rays, and possibly a whale shark, the best time to dive in North or South Male' atolls is from August to November, when the waters are rich with plankton; in Ari Atoll, the best months for seeing them are February to April.

Diving is generally good all year round, but rain, wind and rough sea conditions occur more often during the southwest monsoon season (June–August), and can make getting to some dive sites difficult, if not impossible.

During this time the visibility can vary, occasionally dropping to as low as 10 metres (33 ft). The weather is said to run in two-week cycles, but this

Right: an octopus on a coral head

is not a hard and fast rule as many say the weather patterns are changing. Winds from the northeast in December and January sometimes make it difficult to reach the best dive sites on the outer eastern side of the atolls, but there are always protected areas inside the lagoon and on the sheltered side of the passes where you can dive.

Visibility often exceeds 30 metres (100 ft) and the water temperature is a very comfortable 27–30°C (80–86°F), making heavy wetsuits unnecessary.

Maldivian Diving Rules

The Maldivian government has developed some diving regulations which they believe will help to make diving a safer sport. Decompression diving is forbidden, spear-fishing is illegal and there is a maximum diving depth limit of 30 metres (100 ft). Also, buoyancy compensators (BCs) are a must.

Some dive operators also have their own rules. These usually include a check-out dive: once the instructor is satisfied you are comfortable in the water, you can dive without a guide and usually do not have to follow the group.

In addition, as a further precautionary measure, some resorts ask that on boat dives you surface within one hour or with at least 50 bar (750 psi)

remaining in your tank, whichever comes first. This rule varies, depending on the dive operation, the number of divers in the group and the skill of the divers on board. The taking of corals and other marine life is forbidden, and solo diving is prohibited.

Resort Diving

Resort dive operations typically offer daily morning and afternoon boat dives at sites less than an hour away. Night dives are available on request at most resorts. Resorts with accessible house reefs usually offer unlimited beach diving packages. Some resorts, like Bandos and Ellaidhoo, offer round-the-clock beach diving.

Boat dives are made from local *dhonis*, large and roomy enough to accommodate divers and all their equipment, and they are covered to offer protection from the sun. These boats usually accommodate between four and 20 divers. All-day excursions to remote dive sites are regularly organised and include two boat dives a day, and either a packed lunch or a barbecue on an uninhabited island. Sometimes, a visit to another resort is included.

Resort diving packages: You can get a variety of diving packages at reduced rates – a good idea if you plan to dive for several days. Unlimited diving packages usually include two boat dives a day and unlimited beach diving on the house reef. This option is recommended if your resort has a good house reef, and if you want to do more than two dives a day. The boat fee is often charged separately, but some resorts offer a discount if you purchase one of

Above: buoyancy compensators are compulsory

their diving packages. Some scuba diving is included in the price of a stay at Club Med and at Club Vacanze. On average, a one-dive package will set you back US$35, six dives US$180, 10 dives US$250 and six days of unlimited diving US$230–US$300. The boat fee averages US$10 per trip per person.

Prices for diving packages include tanks and weight belts only, but the resort dive shops have all types of rental equipment. Some also have dive computers, underwater cameras and strobes for rent. However, not all dive operations rent wetsuits. Full equipment rental averages about US$10 a dive for full scuba gear. Individual pieces rent for US$2 per dive and up.

Introductory dive: If you've never dived before, you should try an introductory dive or a resort course. These courses are an introduction to scuba diving, and are designed to get you into the water under the close supervision of a dive instructor so you can see what you have been missing. The introductory dive is just that – a short lecture and demonstration followed by a beach dive in the resort lagoon and on the house reef. This introduction is short, less than half a day, and will help you decide if you would like to pursue the sport. Most resorts offer introductory dives for about US$50, equipment included. If you decide to do a certification course, some resorts will deduct the cost of the introductory dive from the certification course.

Resort course: These are offered by some, but not all, resorts. These courses are longer than the introductory class and include between three and six closely supervised dives. The first three dives are usually done in the lagoon and on the house reef; some diving schools then allow boat dives at their discretion. Prices for resort courses vary from US$200 for

Above: a diving lesson on land
Right: a spotted sweetlip

a three-day, three-dive course to US$350 for a six-day, six-dive course. All equipment is included, but the boat fee is often charged separately.

Some schools offer a certificate and a log book for participating in a resort course, but do remember that this is not a certification for diving and will not be honoured anywhere else in the world. The resort course is meant to serve as an introduction to scuba diving, and if you enjoyed it, your next step is to take a certification course leading to the C-card.

C-card: The major certifying agencies here are PADI, NAUI, SSI and CMAS. Other certifications are available but on a smaller scale. The dive schools have at least one dive instructor, and depending on the resort and the instructors available, courses can be given in all the major European languages as well as Japanese. You will be asked to complete a medical questionnaire before enrolling in the course. The cost for a standard open water certification course is about US$450 (equipment included); an advanced course is about US$320 and includes instruction on night diving, search and recovery, and underwater navigation. Be sure to check with the dive school to see if boat fees are included in the price.

Dive Safaris

A dive safari offers a unique alternative to a resort holiday. Whether it is the appeal of diving remote sites, visiting resorts, villages and uninhabited islands or simply getting away from it all, there is nothing quite like the carefree lifestyle of the live-aboard. All safaris start and end at the airport or

Above: a clown triggerfish
Left: washing equipment after a dive

Male', and typically visit North and South Male' atolls and Felidhoo Atoll for one-week trips and Ari, Lhaviyani and Baa atolls for two-week excursions.

Safari boats are fully equipped yacht-*dhonis* ranging in length from 12 to 30 metres (40–100 ft), with beams of 4–10 metres (13–33 ft). They can accommodate between two and 22 passengers. A dive *dhoni* usually accompanies the main safari boat, storing the compressor, tanks and other essential equipment and ferrying the divers to and from the dive sites.

The price of a dive safari is usually all-inclusive and varies considerably depending on the boat, whether the cabins are air-conditioned, if there is a watermaker, underwater photography processing equipment and/or video monitors and the number of dives offered per day. The lower price range is around US$100 per day while the more expensive boats are around US$350 per day.

The price includes all meals, diving fees, tanks, weights, air fills and the services of a divemaster. Some boats tout 'unlimited diving', but in fact only include two dives per day. Check with your tour operator on prices, services and the diving package and also ask if night diving is included.

There are over 80 registered owners with boats available for dive safaris, and many boats are leased out to foreign dive operators. Among the larger local operators are **Voyages Maldives** (tel: 32-3617; fax: 32-5336; e-mail: voyages@dhivehinet.net.mv), **Phoenix Hotels and Resorts** (tel: 32-3181; fax: 32-5499; e-mail: phoenix@dhivehinet.net.mv) and **Panorama Maldives** (tel: 32-0766; fax: 32-6542; e-mail: panorama@dhivehinet.net.mv).

Two boats catering mainly for the American market are *Manthiri* and *Madivaru 7*, both of which offer luxury facilities, including a bar and up to four dives per day, plus night diving as well. They operate all year round with the exception of June and July during the height of the southwest monsoon. The *Manthiri* is operated by **Sea n' See** in Male' (tel: 32-5634; fax: 32-5633; e-mail: seansee@dhivehinet.net.mv). For bookings in the US, contact **Tropical Adventures** (tel: 1-206-441-3483; fax: 1-206-441-5431; e-mail: dive@divetropical.com) or **Reef and Rainforest** (tel: 1-415-289-1760; fax: 1-415-289-1763; e-mail: rnrtravel@aol.com). *Madivaru 7* is operated by **Seafari Adventures Club** (tel: 32-9338; fax: 32-9362; e-mail: seafari_maldives@iol.it). In the UK, **Sport Abroad** (tel: 44-1306-744-345; fax: 44-1306-744-380; e-mail: info@sportabroad.co.uk) operates the *S/Y Maarana*, a 32-metre (104-ft) sailing yacht offering full board with three dives per day. Another option is *Sea Queen*, operated by **Maldives Scuba Tours**, which offers three dives per day (tel: 32-0981; fax: 32-0981; e-mail: creative@dhivehinet.net.mv).

Drift Diving

Drift diving is the most common method of diving in the Maldives. The strong currents provide an excellent opportunity to explore large sections of reef while gliding carefree along the channel wall. However, care should

Above: the *Manthiri*, a dive-safari boat

be taken when diving in a current as it can increase rapidly in strength during a dive and at some locations, especially during spring tides, the dive may have to be aborted in the interests of diver safety. Always heed the advice of your divemaster as his knowledge will be essential during these times. Diving with an in-going current is generally safer than diving with an out-going one. If there is a strong out-going current, divers need to stay close to the reef and shallow on the outside corners. When it is time to ascend use a surface balloon or parachute for open water safety stops and for signalling your position to the boat crew.

Night Diving

Night dives are often rewarding because of the likelihood of seeing new and different marine life. Fish photography is less difficult at night because fish in their resting state can be approached more easily than during sunlight hours. As the sun goes down, the reef also takes on a different look as familiar reef fish switch into their night-time modes. Wrasses cover themselves with sand, butterfly fish take on a darker night colouration and snuggle up to coral heads, small fish take shelter in crevices and holes, and parrotfish surround themselves with protective mucus bags.

When the retreat is complete, the nocturnal animals emerge. Cup corals colour the reef walls with bright yellow and orange polyps while sea cucumbers lumber across the sand between sea pens. Sweep the reef with your dive light and you will spot soldier fish darting about in their deep red night colours. Examine soft tree corals to find small crabs decorated with bits of sponges and corals for camouflage. Look around for feather stars – curled up during the day, they extend their arms at night to feed.

An intriguing sight on some night dives are the corusgating green lights belonging to the elusive flashlight fish, *Photoblepharon steinitzi*. Found in caverns on moonless nights, this small (10–12 cm/4–5 in) dark fish collects bioluminescent bacteria in a special pouch-like organ located just under each eye. When the pouch is exposed it shows up as a bright green light. The flashlight fish can turn the light on or off at will by covering and uncovering the organ with a flap of skin. The luminous organs are thought to be used to communicate with other flashlight fish, to see and attract prey, and more importantly, to confuse predators.

To see these extraordinary fish, find a convenient spot near the top of a cavern or recess, turn off all lights and wait silently. In a few minutes you will see flashing green lights – first one, then two, then several, and soon a whole sea of them. If you want to photograph these unique fish, use a 1:4 framer with a Nikonos; if using a housed camera, focus on the pocket of light – either way the task is not easy and patience is necessary.

Above: school of collared butterfly fish

diving

Underwater Photography

Plenty of sunshine and fine visibility provide unlimited opportunities for the underwater photographer. Because the subjects range from very small to very large, you should bring close-up and wide-angle equipment. Either way you are sure to find something interesting to capture on film. If you have never tried underwater photography, this is a great place to learn by renting a camera.

The power supply for charging strobes is 220 volts. If your strobe takes ordinary batteries you should remember to bring an ample supply from home. Batteries are available at resorts, but they are expensive and the ones that you need may not always be available.

Kodak and Fuji films are generally available at the resorts; Kodak Underwater Ektachrome is available in Male' and at some of the resorts. Film prices are generally high so it is best to bring a supply from home. Print film and all slide films, except Kodachrome, can be developed and returned to you within a few hours, or a few days, depending on your location. Several resorts, like Bandos and Ellaidhoo, do regular in-house slide processing (E-6). Others process slide film depending on staff expertise and demand. Bandos and Kuramathi also do print processing. Check with your tour operator beforehand to verify the availability of film processing.

Fish Cleaning Stations

The healthy fish life found on Maldivian reefs is due in part to the abundance of cleaner fish and shrimps found here. These cleaners have a

Above: snap-happy diver
Right: a giant clam

mutually beneficial relationship with the fish they clean; they remove dead and diseased tissue, as well as tiny parasitic crustaceans from their customers in exchange for a free meal.

The cleaner you will most often see here is the blue-streak cleaner wrasse, *Labroides dimidiatus*. This small brightly coloured fish dances around its territory, often close to a small coral head, advertising its services. Several species of cleaner shrimps occupy reef crevices and attract customers by waving their long white antennae.

When a fish glides into a cleaning station, the cleaner immediately begins its work while the fish remains motionless, sometimes in a headstand, often changing colour during the cleaning process. Fish, including moray eels with their razor-sharp teeth, open their mouths wide, allowing cleaners to work inside with no fear of being devoured.

Manta Rays and Whale Sharks

Depending on the season, you may chance upon manta rays, and less often, whales or whale sharks. Reaching a length of 14 metres (45 ft) or more, the whale shark is the world's largest fish. Unlike its more notorious relatives, this shark is a plankton eater and can be seen swimming slowly, often with its mouth agape, straining tiny organisms from the water. Manta rays – huge fish that seem to fly through the water – also feed on plankton. With a wingspan that can exceed 6 metres (20 ft), manta rays are an awesome presence when encountered. Far removed from Captain Nemo's leviathans of the deep, these giants are not dangerous, but they are curious – if not harassed, they will sometimes glide over to a group of divers for a closer look before flying off into the deep blue.

Underwater Hazards

It is easy to get caught up in the beauty of the underwater world and forget about the dangers associated with diving. In general, diving in the Maldives is not particularly hazardous, but some things are worth noting.

Several sites are known for their friendly stingrays but care should be taken not to provoke them. When photographing the rays do not get too close as they are a defensive fish with a venomous spine that is extremely painful.

Be careful where you put your hands if touching the reef and look carefully for such things as small moray eels. The

Above: cleaner wrasse feeding off a sweetlip
Left: a whale shark off Ari Atoll

black-cheeked moray hides in small holes and would not hesitate to nip at straying hands. Avoid brushing against corals as some hydroids and fire-coral give a sharp burning sensation when contact is made.

Occasionally, you will see a sea urchin or crown-of-thorns starfish on the reef. Try not to touch them; their spines carry venom, and although their stings are seldom serious, they can cause a certain amount of discomfort. Remember, once you have been pricked, you will not be able to remove the brittle spines and will have to wait for your body to dissolve them naturally.

You may come across a well-camouflaged scorpion fish, or more rarely, a stonefish. Observe this dictum: Don't bother them and they won't bother you. If you spot a lionfish, make sure that you keep your distance; along the length of the fish's spectacular plume-like fins are a series of poisonous glands. If you are accidentally stung by one of these creatures, immediately immerse the wound and the surrounding areas in hot water – as hot as you can endure. The heat will inactivate the venom, but you should also seek medical attention.

Wetsuits are unnecessary for warmth here, but they can make diving a bit more comfortable by protecting you from accidental coral abrasions and the sting of unseen hydroids or stinging plankton. A small bottle of Stingose from your local dive shop quickly neutralises painful hydroid stings as will a hot-water compress.

The combination of sun and sea increases your risk of sunburn. Be sure to use a good sunblock before and after each dive – even when the dive site is only a short boat ride away. And don't forget a wide-brimmed hat and sunglasses.

A final note of caution: make an extra effort to monitor your depth gauge or dive computer regularly during your dives. Because the water is so clear, it is easy to exceed your planned depth limit without realising it.

Dive operators are required to carry a supply of oxygen on the diving *dhoni* for use in the event of emergencies. Dive operations normally have enough oxygen available to support someone until they can get to a decompression chamber.

There is an excellent fully staffed, 24-hour, four-man decompression chamber on Bandos Island which is operated under the auspicies of the *Institut fur Hyperbar und Tauchmedizin* in Donau, Germany. Bandos Clinic is a fully equipped facility with two German medical doctors in residence. There is also a new facility on Kuramathi Tourist Island, with a hyperbaric six-place chamber and a qualified diving doctor always in attendance (tel: 77-3485; email: ktim@kuramathi.com.mv). The Kuramathi Medical Centre also conducts 'fit for diving' examinations. In an emergency the clinics can arrange for a seaplane transfer to their facilities if you are out of *dhoni* or speedboat range.

Right: a giant moray eel in its coral lair

Dive Sites

There are hundreds of well-known dive sites in the Maldives, and new, exciting sites are regularly found. Some have more than one name, and to further confuse things, some reef names are repeated in different areas. Each site offers a unique change of scenery, with particularly stunning changes in marine life. The following sites are samples of the wide variety in the tourist atolls. For more detailed information, find a copy of *Dive Maldives: A Guide to the Maldives Archipelago*, by Tim Godfrey.

North Male' Atoll *(see map, p22)*

HP Reef (Rainbow Reef): This is an exceptional dive with a spectacular reef formation that has been declared a protected marine area. It is a *thila*, 100 metres (328 ft) in length with the top at 9 metres (30 ft). The entire length

of the reef on the southwest side is filled with outcrops of coral, caves and crevices. On the northwest side is a large outcrop of rock divided from the reef by a narrow sand channel. Soft corals and sea fans clutter the sides of the cliffs and overhangs and are nourished by strong currents streaming through Himmafushi Kandu. Large schools of big-eye trevally, blue-fin jack, rainbow runner, barracuda and dog-toothed tuna make this reef a playground for pelagics. Grey reef sharks and eagle rays join in the action and yellow-back fusilier concentrate here in big schools. On the top of the reef you'll see many species of angelfish.

Okobe Thila (Barracuda Thila): This spectacular *thila* has many different features and can be dived in a number of ways. There are three sections of reef to this *thila*, the smallest reef being no more than 10 metres (33 ft) in diameter, while the larger one is about 50 metres (164 ft) in length. A hole in the reef top at 13 metres (43 ft) makes an ideal starting point from where *dhonis* can secure a line. All three reefs are pitted with nooks and crannies, steep ledges, overhangs and caves, providing a veritable feast of marine life for divers. Highlights include several well-camouflaged scorpion fish on the reef top, common lionfish around the ledges, large moray eels in the caves and a thick covering of soft coral on the steep reef walls. A school of tall-fin batfish is usually seen between the reef with schools of barracudas, trevally and dog-toothed tuna.

Above: a dive *dhoni* passing through a channel in the reef
Top Right: the graceful manta ray. **Right:** *dhonis* and divers

In the recesses of the small reef are featherstars, oriental sweetlip, triggerfish, banner fish and squirrelfish.

Manta Point: located on the outside reef of Paradise Island Resort, Manta Point has a world-wide reputation as being one of the most consistent sites for attracting large numbers of manta ray. In 8 metres (26 ft) of water on the southeast corner of the reef are several large coral rocks, which mark the point where mantas converge during the southwest monsoon season. Mantas have been photographed here as early as April and as late as December. These rocks are like one giant cleaner station *(see page 59)* for the mantas. Blue-streak cleaner wrasse, often working in pairs, can be seen swimming out to the hovering mantas to remove old skin and parasites. The mantas circle the rocks waiting for their turn to be cleaned and when finished they swim gracefully up and down the reef feeding on zooplankton in the shallow water.

On a sandy section at 20 metres (66 ft) are a number of white-tip reef sharks, and near the southern tip of the reef is **Lankan Caves.** This is a series of caves and overhangs beginning with a long cave between 10 and 30 metres (33–98 ft). Here, a huge sea fan can be seen at 11 metres (36 ft). There are also parrotfish, surgeonfish, trevally and emperor along this reef.

Note that divers are asked not to chase or harass mantas (the same applies to turtles) as they are easily frightened and less inclined to return in the future. Do not hold the top of the coral rocks or the mantas may think the cleaning station is occupied. Try to stay in a group at a discreet distance. Do not swim around. Stay quiet on the bottom and hold only dead coral.

Furana North/Furana Thila: The eastern side of Full Moon Resort provides excellent diving during the southwest monsoon. The reef top is gnarled

and stunted down to 10 metres (33 ft) because of wave action but there is plenty of fish life. There are a number of diving options. With an in-going current, divers start on the deep outside wall and drift into the atoll on the north side of the island. If the current is gentle, divers can venture out to Furana Thila rising to 8 metres (26 ft) on the north side of the island. There are many surprises here, including nurse sharks, eagle rays, mantas and even whale sharks. Divers can visit caves at 20 and 26 metres (66 and 85 ft) on the southwest side of the *thila*, then drift to the narrow channel to the south side of Kanduoiygiri.

Banana Reef: Named after its shape when viewed from the air, this was one of the first dive sites to be discovered in the Maldives. It is a protected marine area with the top at 3 metres (10 ft) and located close to Club Med. The best diving is at the northeast end where there are large spectacular rocks, caves, deep gutters and precipitous overhangs. The scenery is amazing with predatory fish like shark, barracuda, trevally and black snapper.

The caves have several species of grouper and some, like the snout-spot grouper, have become quite tame, mainly through fish feeding. On the eastern fringe of the reef, in 15 metres (49 ft), is a school of up to 1,000 schooling banner fish. These distinctive fish have long dorsal fins and vertical black and white bands and always inhabit the same area. At times they are so thick that divers can barely see through them. There are also large morays that entwine themselves in green coral trees, pufferfish and many smaller species of wrasse. Cleaner wrasses are common, often swimming well out from the reef and into schools of fusilier. At the western end of the dive, a semi-circular wall drops steeply to 25 metres (82 ft). There is a big cave here, between 10 and 15 metres (33–49 ft), with a multitude of squirrelfish. Many swim upside down and all have big eyes to see in the dark. During strong currents, this concave wall, known as the 'Washing Machine', generates swirling downcurrents attracting grey reef sharks.

Maldive Victory: It started out as a dramatic disaster in the early hours of Friday, 13 February 1981, but the wreck of the *Maldive Victory* quickly became a focal point for divers and was soon hailed as a boon for the local diving industry. The wreck lies upright,

Above: telling diving tales
Right: exploring a wreck

tilted slightly to port in 35 metres (115 ft) of water on the sandy bottom just off Hulhule reef. The 3,500-ton, 83-metre (272-ft) freighter struck the reef at almost full speed after the captain lost his way in the buoy-marked channel. Its hull was badly gashed and it sank within minutes. The 10-year-old freighter was sailing to Male' from Singapore with a full cargo of supplies, mainly for the resort islands. Today, the wreck is stripped bare of anything of value. A buoy has been fixed to the mast at 12 metres (39ft) making descents easier in strong currents. The currents can be treacherous here but once you're on the deck, there is plenty of protection. The entire ship can be comfortably seen in one dive. A good plan is firstly to swim from the mast along the superstructure to the bow. On the way along the deck are three large holds that are wide open and easy to penetrate. A large school of trevally often gathers at the bow. Return to the stern back along the deck and finish at the bridge, where a rope has been tied to the mast at 16 metres (52 ft) to make ascents easier.

South Male' Atoll *(see map, p22)*

Vaadhu Caves: This is one of the most spectacular cave dives in South Male' Atoll. The caves are located on the steep outer reef of Vaadhu Resort. They begin with one large cave that descends from 7 to 25 metres (23–82 ft). There is a long overhang at 30 metres (98 ft) and a narrow cave with a swim-through from 16 to 24 metres (52–79 ft). There are more caves to be found on the northeast side of Vaadhu Resort.

Embudhu Kandu: The entire Embudhu channel has been declared a protected marine area. The south side is an exhilarating 2-km (1¼-mile) long drift dive known as Embudhu Express. With an in-going current, the express steams ahead at full throttle, giving divers the ride of a lifetime. The channel entrance attracts a range of pelagics, large napoleon, eagle rays and grey reef sharks. There are many small caves and overhangs on the corner between 14 and 30 metres (46–98 ft). Under the overhangs are numerous groupers. Inside the channel is one huge cave between 5 and 25 metres (16–82 ft), with a swim-through at 11 metres (36 ft). Many dives start on the outside reef and finish around this cave. It is rich in sea fans and sponges and attracts large morays, angelfish, octopus, lionfish and squirrelfish.

Guradhu South: Another protected marine area, Guradhu South promises a unique diving opportunity for viewing a wide range of marine life. Currents can be extremely strong here, which is one reason why the marine life is so abundant. The outer reef drops off steeply into the open ocean and along the reef are schooling banner fish, turtles and napoleon. Near the corner is a slight ridge extending across the channel at 30 metres (98 ft), where big

Right: a sabre squirrelfish

schools of fusilier, rainbow runner, tuna, trevally and grey reef sharks congregate. Inside the channel are caves and overhangs between 5 and 25 metres
(16–82 ft) and pinnacles of rock on the deeper slopes. Current flows both
in and out of the channel, which opens up many diving alternatives. With
an out-going current, a school of eagle rays often hover inside at around
25 metres (82 ft) while on the bottom at 30 metres (98 ft) are white-tipped
reef sharks. Divers stay shallow on the outside corner at these times, coming up to a long cave at 16 metres (52 ft), where there are fans, featherstars,
sponges and soft coral, before rounding the corner away from the current.
With an in-going current, divers can venture deeper onto the ridge into the
channel to view the sharks.

Ari Atoll *(see map, p34)*

Rasdhoo-Madivaru: This site has a reputation for scalloped hammerhead
sharks, *Sphyrna lewini*. It is from the deep waters on the outside wall off

this island in Rasdhoo Atoll that divers
can get a good look at these unusual sharks.

Maaya Thila: This submerged reef
rising to 6 metres (20 ft) has been
declared a protected marine area. It is
the white-tip reef shark capital of the
atoll, with dozens of them circling the
reef at any one time. This dive is a fish-
watchers delight with stonefish and
angler fish commonly seen.

Halaveli Wreck: The wreck is a 38-
metre (124-ft) cargo vessel which sunk
in 1991. It sits upright with the deck at 20
metres (66 ft) and the bottom on sand at
28 metres (92 ft). Apart from the wreck

Above: school of silvery fish above a reef
Left: brightly coloured sea sponge

itself, the main attraction here are four large stingrays up to 1½ metres (5 ft) across that have made this their home.

Mushimasmingili Thila (Fish Head): The presence of a large school of grey reef sharks, combined with the favourable underwater scenery and the variety of marine life, have given this reef the reputation of being among the 10 best dive sites in the world. The square-shaped reef is about 80 metres (262 ft) wide and rises to 10 metres (33 ft). It is a protected marine area. Divers tend to stay more shallow at Fish Head, hovering around the reef edge at about 15 metres (49 ft), as this gives the best all-round view of a family of about 20 resident grey reef sharks, usually seen on the up-current side of the reef. The advantage Fish Head has over other shark-watching sites is that the habits of the sharks can be observed at close range from a secure position on any part of the reef. Photographers will also get good opportunities to photograph these graceful predators.

Kudarah Thila: One of the most exceptional diving areas in Ari Atoll is in the 5-km (3-mile) wide channel between the islands of Dhigurah and Dhagathi, where several *thilas* are located near the outer rim of the atoll. One of them is Kudarah Thila, now a protected marine area. The reef top is at 14 metres (46 ft), and on the deeper slopes are great expanses of large sea fans that sway as one in the current.

Addu Atoll *(see map, p4)*

Just south of the equator, and about 550 km (340 miles) south of Male', is Addu Atoll, the southernmost atoll in the Maldives. It is a small atoll, about 15 km (9 miles) across, with deep water all round and only four channels. Divers who expect an abundance of reef fish may be a little disappointed, but those who want to see wrecks, large manta rays, sharks, turtles and generally big fish all year round, will be absolutely delighted.

British Loyalty: The 5,583-ton oil tanker, *British Loyalty*, was torpedoed on 9 March 1944 by a submarine that had fired through a gap in the submarine nets blocking Gan island *(see page 14)*. The ship was damaged but not sunk and remained inside the atoll for the remainder of the war. It was finally scuttled on 5 January 1946, before the British withdrew from Gan. The 140-metre (459-ft) wreck lies on its starboard side with the bottom at 33 metres (108 ft). The port side is at 16 metres (52 ft) and the bow points almost directly north. The propeller is at 28 metres (92 ft) and is covered in big bushy black coral trees. In front of the engine room are two large holes, one on the deck, the other on the keel. These holes – most likely caused when the torpedo exploded – are so big that divers can swim through them without any trouble at all.

Right: a hawksbill turtle

Leisure *Activities*

SHOPPING

If you are a shopping fanatic, the Maldives is not really the place for you. The tourist resorts usually have a boutique where you can find the essentials, but many of the souvenir items on sale are also available in Male' at much lower prices. So part of the fun of going on an excursion to the capital *(see page 42)* is the chance to browse among the rows of colourful and quaint little shops in **Chandhani Bazaar**, a nickname given to the sector bounded by Haveeree Higun, Chandhani Magu and Fareedhee Magu.

Ironically, most of the items on sale here are imported from Sri Lanka, India, Indonesia or Thailand. There are few items that are Maldivian in origin because of the high labour costs on the islands.

Most of the tourist shops in Male' are open from 9am to 11pm, but they close for a few minutes several times each day for prayers. If you are already inside, you can stay put. On Fridays, the shops are open only after 2pm. English is spoken at most shops, as is a smattering of German, Italian, French and Japanese. Bargaining is a must as there seems to be no fixed prices for the goods, and much depends on your bargaining skills and patience. You can often save as much as 30 percent with a little haggling. As one signboard in a store boldly states: 'We are always open for discussion.'

Replica Dhonis

Among the most popular local handicrafts on sale are replica *dhonis* made of wood, coral or mother-of-pearl. These miniatures can measure anywhere from 30 cm (1 ft) to 1 metre (3 ft) in length, complete with oars and sails. Although some shops sell *dhonis* made from black coral, you are advised not to purchase these as it only encourages further degradation of the precious coral reefs. In any case, most countries restrict the import of black coral and tortoise shell in accor-

dance with the Convention on International Trade of Endangered Species (CITES) agreements. Go for the wooden *dhonis* instead – **M Orchid Uffa** on Faamudheyri Magu has a good selection.

Shark's Teeth

Keen fishermen may like to pick up a set or two of shark's jaws as a memento of their trip. Having lost their bite, you will find displays of gaping jaws on the walls of numerous tourist shops. Recommended are **Schist** and **The Shop** (tel: 32-3610) on Fareedhee Magu. Costing between US$2 and US$250, these items make interesting pieces.

Ethnic Jewellery

Many of the shops around the bazaar have interesting collections of old silver and antique jewellery originating from India and Sri Lanka. Check around for the best prices and selections.

Reed Mats

Another local handicraft item worth considering are the unique reed mats, or *thundu kunaa*, with their interesting black and brown motifs. These mats are naturally dyed and

Left: fine dining on the sand
Right: shark's teeth for sale

often used as prayer mats and bed covers by the local people. Unfortunately, the mats are difficult to find as they are not produced in huge quantities. The best examples come from Huvadhoo Atoll.

Lacquerware

Perhaps the most popular souvenir from the Maldives is a type of lacquerware known as *lielaa jehun*, which comes from the island of Thuladhoo in Baa Atoll. Traditionally made from local wood, the lacquerware is crafted into items such as walking sticks, boxes, trays and vases. The most impressive are the large circular dishes with elaborate designs on their lids that are used for festive occasions. If you have visited the National Museum in Male', you will have seen many fine examples used for royal functions in the past. Handpainted and carved with yellow, red and black floral patterns, *lielaa jehun* products can be found decorating the shelves of many Maldivian households. **Orchid Ufaa** (tel: 32-5430), on the corner of Orchid and Faamudheyri Magu, has a nice collection of lacquerware, from small boxes to large, intricately detailed pieces. Prices range from US$8 to US$500.

Clothes

T-shirts are one of the best bargains in Male'. Many shops hand-paint fish portraits on to T-shirts and some will even custom-make designs to your specifications. Among the shops selling tourist beachware in day-glo colours, **Lemon** (tel: 32-3390), a little shop on Chandhani Magu, stands out. Run by a Maldivian and his Japanese wife, Lemon carries an assortment of colourful T-shirts embossed with designs such as coconut trees, fish, *dhonis* and sails. Though more expensive and with fixed prices, the T-shirts here are of better quality and the designs unique.

The *batik* you see in the stores is not Maldivian but Indonesian and Sri Lankan. The Maldives does produce a traditional brown and cream cloth known as *feyli*, but it is very difficult to find. If you wish to buy *batik*, check out **Bamboo** (tel: 32-2354), one of the first few shops on Chandhani Magu. This store also carries a good range of leather bags of reasonable quality and prices. Another shop that specialises in *batik* is **Royal Arts** on Orchid Magu.

If the heat should get to you – and it probably will – you can probably find all that you want in the cool comfort of **Najaah Artpalace** (tel: 32-2372), on the first and second floors of the MHA Building at the junction of Chandhani Magu and Orchid Magu. This is the largest and most complete of shops. It also has a good collection of postcards and books on the Maldives.

Essentials and Bargains

There are a number of general stores along Orchid Magu and Chandhani Magu in Male' where you can find essentials such as soap, shampoo and toothpaste. For a wider selection, check out the larger supermarkets, such as **STO** on Orchid Magu or **Fantasy** on Fareedhee Magu, where many expats do their shopping.

STO is especially interesting for its display of items used by Maldivians. Cotton sarongs imported from India are fun for beachwear; look for "100 by 100" grade for the softest cotton weave. Here you'll also find the sun-dried fish pieces known as 'Maldive fish', an essential seasoning for curry. And look out for canned tuna fish produced in the Maldives; it is particularly good.

The **People's Choice** electronics showroom on Chandhani Magu is great for low-priced gadgetry (only 5 percent tax), and there are good watches at **Reefside**, around the corner on Orchid Magu. When you leave the islands, don't forget the shopping arcade on the first floor of the airport for duty-free perfume and alcohol.

Above: making lacquer paste, which will be turned into traditional lacquerware

EATING OUT

One of the most common complaints among visitors at resorts is the amount of fish served at mealtimes. Bear in mind, however, that fish is the staple food for the local people – the Maldivian dried fish can be cooked an umpteen number of ways – and almost everything else has to be imported from neighbouring countries. And to be fair, the food served at most resorts is above average, with diners usually being offered a choice between a Western menu and a local curry and rice meal. At upmarket resorts like the Four Seasons, Banyan Tree and Kurumba, meat (even pork) is never in short supply. In most resorts, an international buffet is often part of the standard offering, to cater to the varied tastes of the many nationalities. A wide range of alcohol and beer is sold at the bars in the resorts, though this is prohibited on all the inhabited islands and in Male'. However, the best bar in the Maldives is very close to Male': the **Captain's Fun Pub** (open 11am–1am daily) at the Hulhule Island Hotel on the airport island.

Apart from the familiar fish curry and rice, few tourists ever get a chance to try genuine Maldivian fare. Excursions to Male' are generally scheduled so that guests are back at the resorts for the main meals of the day, but after a week of endless buffets, resort food can get a little monotonous. For the curious, an excursion to Male' can serve as an eye-opener to the delights of Maldivian cuisine.

Teahouses and Maldivian Food

Stepping into a local teahouse to savour a Maldivian meal with the locals can be a novel experience. Teahouses are found on almost every street in Male'. Oddly, 'tea-time' in the Maldives can fall anywhere between morning and midnight.

The teahouse, like the fish market, is the domain of men: women are rarely seen. You will find well-dressed office workers having their meals alongside *sarong*-clad fishermen seated on long wooden benches. Many of the teahouses are open for breakfast early in the morning and close at about midnight. In the evening, they become popular hangouts for young Maldivians since nightlife and entertainment are practically non-existent in Male'.

There are no menus in the teahouses. Until mid-1997, an assortment of snacks or *hedhikaa* were laid out on every table in small portions. You were only charged for what you consumed, though it always amazed the uninitiated that the waiter was able to remember what was eaten and by whom. Since 1997, however, the teahouses have all been self-service.

Above: barbecue on the beach

You will notice that the locals eat with their hands, but remember, if you plan to do like them, always use your right hand to pick at the food and your left to serve cutlery.

For a few *rufiyaa* you can have a hearty meal washed down with a cup of very sweet tea with milk. If you find the tea too sweet, tell the waiter to hold the sugar. Most of the snacks are made with a mixture of fish or meat, and combined with coconut and wheat or rice flour, and then deep-fried. Many of the *hedhikaa* are hot and spicy, like *kuli bokibaa*, a spicy fish cake with garlic and chillies; and *gula*, a round fish ball mixed with coconut and onion. There is also *bajiya*, made of fish and onions and formed into small triangular shapes; and *foni bokibaa*, a baked sweet pastry with fried onions.

Another savoury snack is *bis keemiya*, a combination of cabbage, onions and eggs. For the sweet-toothed, there is *folhi*, a flour and sugar mixture; *donkeo kajuru,* fried banana-flavoured balls; and *keyku*, a sweet fluffy sponge cake. For lunch and dinner, there is always a separate table on which dishes of curried fish, vegetables and rice are placed. Popular among the locals is the plain flat bread, or *roshi*, torn into small pieces and dipped into curries. For breakfast, Maldivians enjoy *mas huni*, tuna fish pieces with grated coconut, sliced onions, chilli and lime juice. This is eaten wrapped in *roshi*.

Although most teahouses serve almost identical food, a popular choice in Male' is the one at the **Market Hotel**, situated above the Fish Market, where you can watch *dhonis* coming in and the busy street below. **The Queen of the Night**, on Bodu Thakurufaanu Magu near the Nasandhura Palace Hotel, has one of the biggest selections of local delicacies in the city. For tasty fried noodles and snacks, look out for **Camy Cool Spot** on Majeedhee Magu. Among the locals, the **Buruzu Hotel** near the Clock Tower, and **Hotel Dhanbuma** on Faamudheyri Magu are very popular.

For more substantial fare at a similarly low cost, try **Quench** on Majeedhee Magu, **Newport** on the waterfront and the **Evening Café** on Orchid Magu. Several small eateries have also opened up around Male's southern harbour, and they are lively at night as well as good for a lunch break.

Restaurants in Male'

If eating in a local teahouse is not exactly your cup of tea, there are several restaurants serving non-Maldivian food in Male'. Compared to the local teahouses, where you can have a meal for about Rf20, the restaurants will seem like a costly affair. The price categories given are based on an average meal for two persons and are divided as follows:

Inexpensive = under US$15
Moderate = US$15–US$30
Expensive = over US$30

Central Hotel Restaurant
Rahdebai Magu
Tel: 31-7755
The newest and largest hotel in town has a good restaurant with a very wide selection of food. Open daily 6.30am–midnight. *Moderate*

Gadhoo Seafood and Grill Restaurant
Hulhule Island Hotel
Tel: 33-0888
On the nearby airport island rather than in Male' itself, Gadhoo has a good menu of unusual starters and meat dishes. Adjoining it is the Faru Coffee House (open 24 hours) with European, Japanese and Asian cuisine. *Expensive.*

Ground Six Restaurant
Relax Inn, Ameer Ahmed Magu
Tel: 31-4531
On the top floor of the Relax Inn, this restaurant serves Western and Asian cuisine and has a lovely view of the harbour. Open daily 6.30am–midnight. *Moderate*

Above: the weather in the Maldives is perfect for outdoor dining

Haruge
Bodu Thakurufaanu Magu
(beside the artificial beach)
Tel: 33-7733
A superb, open-sided, breeze-cooled, upstairs restaurant (downstairs is a snack bar), with slightly arty décor but an unpretentious ambience and good food for lunch or dinner. Open 8.30am–1am. *Inexpensive.*

Kam Hotel Restaurant
Ameer Ahmed Magu
Tel: 32-0611
This agreeable restaurant serves generous portions of tasty Chinese and Western food. Buffet on Thursday night. Open daily 6.30am–11pm. *Expensive*

Park View Restaurant
Chandhani Magu
Tel: 32-8106
Considered to be the most expensive in the city, the setting is rather posh by Male' standards. The menu offers a wide selection of Continental, Indian and Chinese dishes. Open daily 10am–11pm, Fridays 1.30–3pm and 6–11pm. *Expensive*

Raiveriya
155 Majeedhee Magu
Tel: 31-8696
Part of the Villingili View Inn (on the west side of Male'), this restaurant serves meals in its patio garden and upstairs in the Sea View Room. Open 6.30am–1am. *Moderate.*

Seagull Café
Corner of Fareedhee Magu and Chandhani Magu
Tel: 32-3332
A deluxe ice-cream parlour with sandwiches, salads and light meals for lunch in a garden setting. Good toilets too. Open daily 8.30am–8pm. *Moderate.*

Symphony
Athama Goalhi
Tel: 32-6277
This restaurant (open 10am–midnight) and its sister establishments of **Synthiana** (*Ameenee Magu; tel: 31-5055*; open 10am–1am) and **Symphonic** (*M Unigas Magu; tel: 32-2362*; open 11am–1am) are cosy places with local and Western dishes, including steaks, served swiftly and pleasantly. *Inexpensive.*

Thai Wok
Ameer Ahmed Magu
Tel: 31-0007
The only Thai restaurant in Male', with authentic food cooked by a Thai chef. Open daily noon–3.30pm and 7.30–11.30pm. Smoking area and VIP room available. *Moderate.*

Trends
Nasandhura Palace Hotel,
Bodu Thakurufaanu Magu
Tel: 32-3380
A charming open-air restaurant serving a variety of Western and Asian dishes. Open daily 24 hours. *Moderate*

Twin Peaks Italian Restaurant
Orchid Magu
Tel: 32-7830
Run by Italians, Twin Peaks serves some of the best pasta and pizzas this side of Italy, plus tasty homemade ice cream and pastries. Also available are meat and fish dishes and a good selection of salads. Highly recommended. Open daily 9am–3pm and 6–11pm, Fridays 6–11pm. *Expensive*

Right: mouthwatering seafood

WATER SPORTS AND OTHER ACTIVITIES

Brilliant sunshine, optimum water temperature and excellent visibility make the Maldives an ideal destination for a whole range of water sports such as windsurfing, waterskiing, catamaran sailing, fishing and snorkelling. The shallow, calm waters that surround many islands provide the perfect learning grounds for novices starting off on their first lessons. The seas are calmest from November to April, but there are also calm periods to be found in the less settled months from May to October.

Surfing, Sailing and Skiing

Resorts normally charge an hourly, daily or weekly rate for the use of their sports facilities. Some, like Club Med, offer free use of windsurfing boards, catamarans, canoes and other equipment in their resort package. Beginner and advanced courses are generally conducted in English. For a higher fee, private tuition can be arranged. Most resorts offer almost the same variety of water sports although only a few offer water-skiing and parasailing. If these are deciding factors in choosing a resort make sure you check with your travel agent when booking your package.

Windsurfing

Serious windsurfing buffs may find the Maldives a little disappointing. The winds are moderate for most of the year, except in July and August when winds of over 20 knots will send your adrenaline racing. Unfortunately, this is also smack in the middle of the rainy season. Without a surf, it is plain slalom, speed sailing and cruising. Experienced windsurfers should choose resorts with large lagoons, like Reethi Rah and Ari Beach, or else venture beyond the house reefs into open waters. However, the moderate winds during the dry season and the calm lagoons are perfect conditions for beginners and novices of the sport.

One of the hazards of windsurfing is the presence of coral heads in the shallow water. A good windsurfing instructor will point out these spots to you; if not, ask. For added protection, you should wear booties to protect yourself against coral cuts. On average, a basic course will set you back US$200, and private lessons US$35 an hour.

If you want to try the exciting new sport of **kite-surfing** (like windsurfing, but with a kite instead of a sail), head for the Reethi Beach Resort in Baa Atoll, where Waterworld (www.h2o-world.net) teaches a basic course costing US$330, and offers equipment rental at US$35 an hour.

Catamaran Sailing

Cutting through the waves with the wind in your face can be an exhilarating experience. Note that at some resorts, for safety reasons, staff will not rent out catamarans unless you produce a certificate proving your ability. Alternatively, hitch a ride with someone who is qualified. Rentals by the hour average

US$35, and US$130 for the whole day. A basic course will cost you about US$250, while private lessons are US$45 an hour.

Water-skiing

Some, but not many, resorts offer water-skiing. A good number of resorts do not allow it because of environmental reasons – some say it scares the fish away. If you want to ski, verify availability before booking your package. The cost for one round of water-skiing is about US$18.

Parasailing

Not all resorts offer this sport because of the risks involved and the skilled staff required. For the uninitiated, parasailing involves wearing a body harness with an attached parachute and being lifted up over water while tethered to a moving speedboat. After you've being carried aloft for about 15 minutes, the boat comes to a gradual stop, you lose height and gently land on the beach. Some would hesitate to call it a sport, as absolutely no skill is required of the participant; the only pre-requisite is that you don't suffer from vertigo! Check with your tour operator for resorts currently offering parasailing. The average cost is US$50 per ride.

Surfing

The Maldives is an undiscovered surfer's paradise. There are classic reef breaks and tube riding when the wind is right. The season is from April to November, which coincides with the off-season, when room rates are lowest.

Young Maldivians have taken to surfing in a big way and can be seen every day off the southeast corner of Male', just beyond the artificial beach, paddling out to wait for the right wave to surf back to shore. Waves are usually around 2 metres (7 ft) high.

Resorts closest to the good surf areas are Four Seasons, Full Moon, Lhohifushi and Paradise Island. Surfing holiday packages are sometimes offered by **Sun Travels & Tours** (tel: 32-5975; fax: 32-0419; web: www.sunholidays.com).

Dhoni Sailing

Sail-*dhonis* are small, traditional wooden boats with triangular sails. They usually take a maximum of six people. Sailing trips take guests around the nearby waters. On a windy day, this can be a relaxing and enjoyable way to pass an afternoon. A minimum of two people is required. Trips cost about US$12 an hour.

Snorkelling

With an abundance of healthy reefs within a few metres of the surface, the Maldives is a snorkeller's delight. Check beforehand that your resort has a good 'house reef' (ie easily accessible from the resort beach). If not, *dhonis* can ferry guests to nearby reefs for a fee, or as part of an island-hopping excursion, or combined with a picnic.

Snorkelling is easy as no cumbersome gear or specialised training is needed: all you need is a mask, fins and a snorkel, and lots of sunblock on your back. Gazing into the warm, clear water, you will see hard corals in shades of pink, blue and lavender.

The brilliant colours are visible to the naked eye only when you snorkel in shallow water. Sea water absorbs colour as light passes through it, so the deeper you go, the less colour you see. Although your eyes will compensate for this loss, the colours you see will always be diminished unless you restore them with a camera strobe or an underwater light.

In sandy areas, look for groups of black-and-white striped damselfish that hover above small corals, and for multi-coloured wrasses poking around in the sand for a meal of small crustaceans. Because these fish have no fear of people, snorkelling in the Maldives is like swimming through an aquarium.

If you see a lot of massive corals, look for parrotfish that munch these corals with their beak-like teeth in order to get at the algae they contain. Try to spot giant clams in the sand and smaller ones embedded in the massive corals.

To get your adrenaline pumping, swim out to the end of the reef and have a look over the edge, where the reef drops dramatically away. You may see an orange cloud of fairy basslets near the reef, groups of gold-lined glowfish and all the way down, in the deep blue, giant pink sea fans that decorate the deeper reefs. Here, larger fish like sweetlips, jacks and snappers, and schools of fusiliers glide past.

Left: sailing a catamaran on gentle seas

Snorkelling gear is available for rent from the dive shop at your resort for US$8–10 a day. If you have never snorkelled before, someone at the dive shop will explain the technique. If you want to capture these beautiful reefs on film, Kodak and Fuji have disposable underwater cameras made just for snorkellers that are good to 3 metres (10 ft). They come loaded with 24-exposure, ISO 400 film and are available at resorts for about US$20 each. The film can be processed and returned to you within a few hours or days, depending on your resort.

Snorkelling is good fun, but a note of caution – the combination of tropical sun and sea can give you bad sunburn. You should always use a waterproof sun block with a high Sun Protection Factor (SPF), especially on the back of your legs and shoulders, and wear a T-shirt for additional protection.

Never bring up any of the corals, shells or other marine life. When taken out of their environment, these animals soon die and lose all their colour, and they start to smell.

Fishing

Although fishing is the economic lifeline of the Maldivians, fishing for big game fish as a sport is relatively unknown. There is, as yet, no organisation in the Maldives that promotes sport-fishing, although this obviously has great potential with the teeming waters all around. Most resorts offer a range of day and night *dhoni* fishing activities for guests.

You can fish all year round in the Maldives, but rough sea conditions from June to September can cause last-minute cancellations. On the eastern side of the atolls choppy seas can be a problem in December and January. Night fishing is quite popular among resort guests as there is little to do in the evenings. Night fishing times can vary but the length of the trip is usually three hours or less. The expeditions are usually followed by barbecues on the beach, or else the fish is prepared at the resort for dinner.

Daytime trips generally go offshore to deeper waters where the catch is bonito, barracuda, yellowfin tuna and the like. Line-fishing and trolling are the standard techniques. At night you can expect to fish closer to the reef where line-fishing is the norm. The catch here is usually grouper and other reef fish. On average, a half-day trip by *dhoni* will cost US$35 and a night trip US$25 per person for a minimum of four to 10 participants.

Some resorts offer deep-sea fishing from a speedboat; others use modified yacht-*dhonis* for offshore fishing trips. These boats take four to six people and go offshore in search of big barracuda, sailfish and, occasionally, marlin. A full day or night of deep-sea fishing costs US$400–600. Half-day excursions are available for about US$350. Check with your tour operator for availability if deep-sea fishing is a must for you.

Island-hopping

A day out on an uninhabited island is the perfect getaway for those who want to soak up the beauty and serenity of an isolated island without any modern intrusions.

Every resort and several travel agents in Male' organise full-day picnic excursions to selected uninhabited islands. These excursions include transportation by *dhoni* or speedboat to a nearby uninhabited island, where you can spend the day lazing around on a white sandy beach, snorkelling, reef fishing or visiting other nearby isolated islands. A barbecue lunch of grilled fish, sandwiches, salads and fresh fruit is usually served on the beach.

Such island excursions generally leave at about 9am and return you to your resort by 5pm. Some resorts prefer to organise island trips with transportation provided by seaplane. Prices vary with the distance and mode of transportation used.

Seaplane Excursions

Two seaplane companies operate in the Maldives, primarily to ferry guests from the airport to resorts in Ari, Baa, Dhaalu, Faafu, Lhaviyani, Meemu and Raa atolls, and back again. The fare is usually built into a holiday package, and works out at about US$120 one-way for independent travellers.

Both companies operate Male' shopping excursions, with the prices set by the resorts. Short photography flights can also be arranged for a minimum of 10 passengers at US$55–US$75 per passenger. Fly and dive packages, co-ordinated through resorts' diving schools, are also popular.

Both companies use 16-seat Twin Otter aircraft with floats attached. Every flight has two pilots and one cabin attendant. Planes generally taxi up to an anchored raft landing stage for passengers to reach their resort, although sometimes they ride the surf up to the beach on uninhabited islands. The seaplane terminal is on Hulhule airport island, opposite the international terminal.

Maldivian Air Taxi (MAT), PO Box 2023, Male'; tel: 31-5201; fax: 31-5203; web: www. mataxi. com; e-mail: mataxi@dhive-hinet.net.mv;

Trans Maldivian Airways (TMA), PO Box 2079, Male'; tel: 32-5708; fax: 32-3161; e-mail: mail@tma.com.mv

Cruises

Cruise safaris are gaining popularity as an alternative to staying at a resort. There are a number of tour operators in Male' that organise cruises. Prices vary with the kind of boat used and the number of people in the group. At the high end are cruise ships and luxury yachts with air-conditioning, individual showers and posh fittings. If your budget is limited, consider a converted *dhoni* with more basic facilities. Yacht-*dhonis* – a cross between a cargo boat and a cabin cruiser – are the most popular among cruise-operators. Most operators will include diving for an extra fee. For information on diving safaris, *see page 56*.

Universal Enterprises (tel: 32-3080) runs cruises on *Atoll Explorer*, a 20-cabin vessel that is popular among those not solely intent on diving, although there is a diving school on board.

Voyages Maldives (tel: 32-3617; fax: 32-5336; e-mail: info@voyages.com.mv), one of the largest tour operators in the Maldives, offers a variety of packages for cruising. An eight-day trip begins from the airport or Male', cruising to uninhabited islands, fishing villages and resort islands in North and South Male' and other permitted atolls. The trip can be tailored to suit individual groups. Voyages Maldives has several yacht-*dhonis* for hire. They all have private cabins, toilets, fresh-water showers and cater for 10 to 14 passengers. The cost of full-board accommodation is US$60–90 per person a day, depending on group size and boat.

The *Muna*, a beautiful double-masted sailing ship, runs seven-day cruises in North and South Male' atolls. It is 24 metres (79 ft) long and takes between six and twelve passengers in six cabins. Call 44-3157 or e-mail meeru@dhivehinet.net.mv for details.

Charter Boats

While local tour operators will make up groups of strangers to join semi-scheduled cruises, boats can also be chartered for exclusive use. Costs vary according to the size and type of vessel, but would usually start at around US$2,000 a day.

Charters of various sizes, from small, two-cabin vessels up to the luxury 11-cabin motor yacht *Maleesha* (which comes with fax and e-mail facilities as well as dive and fishing centres), can be arranged through **Inner Maldives** (tel: 32-6309; fax: 33-0884; e-mail: intermal@dhivehinet.net.mv; web: www.innermaldives.com.mv).

Above: holidaymakers arriving by seaplane

Practical Information

GETTING THERE

European charter airlines such as LTU, Condor, Corsair and Monarch bring the majority of visitors to the Maldives. Recently, however, non-stop scheduled flights from London, Paris and Zurich were introduced by Sri Lankan Airlines, who also operate a direct service from Tokyo. Emirates Airlines also run scheduled flights from Europe, but you have to change planes in Dubai.

Regular connections from Asia are by Sri Lankan Airlines from Colombo, Singapore Airlines from Singapore and Malaysian Airlines from Kuala Lumpur. Air Seychelles has introduced a service from the Seychelles to Male' and Bombay and back, while Indian Airlines operates flights from Trivandrum. Travellers from North America can connect via Europe, Dubai, Tokyo or Singapore. All international flights touch down at Male' International Airport on Hulhule Island.

TRAVEL ESSENTIALS

When to Visit

The best time to visit the Maldives is during the dry northeast monsoon from late December to April. This period is marked by lots of sunshine, blue skies and little rainfall. The sea is also calm and water visibility is at its best, making for good diving. Although high-season rates start in November, this month and December can be quite rainy and windy. The southwest monsoon runs from May to November. This is the wet season and the weather is less predictable, with heavy rainfall sometimes accompanied by very strong winds. The sea can also get pretty rough. Although the two periods are quite distinct, there may be weeks of sunshine in August and September and the occasional shower in February and March. The temperature, however, hardly varies throughout the year.

Passports and Visas

Make sure that your passport is valid for at least six months and that you have a return air ticket and US$25 per day for the duration of your stay. A 30-day visa is issued upon arrival. Nationals from Bangladesh, India, Pakistan and Italy are issued 90-day visas on arrival. Visa extensions can be obtained from the Department of Immigration in Male'.

Customs

The customs check at Male' International Airport is a thorough affair, with all baggage X-rayed on arrival, after which passengers are often asked to open their bags for a closer inspection. This is a Muslim country and local sensitivities must be observed. No alcohol, pork products, pornographic material or idols of worship are allowed into the country. Any alcohol in your posession when you arrive will be held in bond for you to retrieve on departure. (Don't worry, though – the resorts all have well-stocked bars.) Firearms, ammunition and drugs are also prohibited. Visitors are allowed to bring in tobacco, but only for personal consumption. The export of tortoiseshell and corals, except in ornamental form, is illegal, and offenders will face heavy penalties.

Left: getting around Male' the easy way
Right: surfing is becoming popular

Health and Vaccinations

Yellow fever vaccinations are required for visitors coming from affected areas. There is no malaria in the Maldives, and nearly all the resorts have successfully suppressed the breeding of mosquitoes. However, it is not a bad idea to bring along a mosquito repellent. There is generally little problem with food but some visitors may suffer from an upset stomach because of the change in diet. Avoid drinking unboiled water during your stay. Drinking water is supplied at all the resorts and bottles of mineral water are also readily available.

Sun-worshippers should guard against over-exposure, especially those coming from temperate climates. Allow your body time to acclimatise by spending only a small amount of time in the sun for the first few days. Always use a sunblock with a high SPF, stay out of the sun during the hottest hours of the day – between noon and 3pm – and drink lots of water to prevent dehydration.

Weather

The Maldives has a tropical climate, with daily temperatures ranging between 25 and 32°C (77–90°F). At night, the temperature only drops by about 3 degrees. Water temperature is a balmy 27–30°C (80–86°F) all year round and is ideal for most water sports. Humidity is high, about 75–80 percent, though this is made tolerable by the cool ocean breezes.

Clothing

Lightweight cotton clothes are best. During the rainy season, a light raincoat and a foldable umbrella may come in handy. While resort dressing is informal, visitors to Male' and fishing villages should dress with some decorum, especially when visiting mosques. Women should cover their thighs, avoid see-through clothes and bikini-tops. T-shirts and shorts are quite acceptable for men, but keep the torso covered. Sunbathing in the nude is not allowed anywhere.

Electricity

All resorts have generators that provide power 24 hours a day. Electricity is 220 volts AC at 50Hz. The standard round-pin European plug is increasingly being replaced by square pin models.

Time Differences

The Maldives is five hours ahead of GMT. Some resorts set their clocks ahead to allow guests to enjoy a longer day. This practice also allows ample time for airport transfers, especially for resorts further from the airport.

GETTING ACQUAINTED

Geography

The Maldive islands are part of the Laccadives-Chagos ridge that runs north-south for over 2,000km (1,200 miles) in the central Indian Ocean. Located south of India and 670 km (416 miles) west of Sri Lanka, the Maldives is a double strand of atolls straddling the equator and stretching over 800 km (500 miles) long and 130 km (80 miles) wide. For a detailed explanation of atoll formation, *see pages 52–3*. The land area of the Maldives is less than 1 percent of its territory and consists of 1,190 small islands (and numerous sand bars and coral outcrops), most of which are less than 2 metres (7ft) above sea level. Approximately 200 islands are inhabited, and at present, another 87 are leased out as resorts. The rest are uninhabited. Male', the capital island, is centrally located and is the focal point for administrative affairs. The atolls have been regrouped into 19 administrative atolls, and noted by a change of name.

Above: Maldivian men often wear sarongs

Island Aviation Ltd provides regular service to the outlying islands, but inter-island transport is usually limited to travel by *dhoni* (motorised launch) or ferry. Sailing from Male' to the southernmost atoll can take two days or more. Transport between resort islands is by boat or seaplane.

Government and Economy

The government is divided into three levels – that of island, atoll and nation. Each inhabited island is ruled by a *kateeb*, or island chief, responsible for administrative matters and the general management of his island, including any nearby uninhabited islands. The *kateeb* reports to the *atolu verin*, or atoll chief, by radio each day. The atoll chief is in charge of the economic and political welfare of the atoll. He is assisted by a group of *gazis* who attend to judicial matters.

Overseeing all the atolls is the nation's central government in Male', with the President at the helm. Every five years a candidate for President is chosen from a list of nominees by the Citizens' Majlis, comprising two representatives from each atoll, two representatives from Male' and eight Presidential appointees. The President is then elected by national referendum.

Lacking land resources, the Maldives is instead blessed with rich waters and beautiful islands that account for the country's two main industries – fishing and tourism. Fishing is by far the main occupation, employing 22 percent of the working population. Fish exports form over 70 percent of total exports. Tourism is the most dynamic sector of the economy and the highest foreign revenue earner. Tourist arrivals are over 400,000 per year. Since the establishment of the first resort in 1972, 87 resorts islands have been developed. Resorts are concentrated in North and South Male' and Ari atolls, but in 1998, 14 islands outside these atolls were allocated for resort development. This is part of an effort to spread the fruits of tourism to the more remote atolls.

Religion

Islam is the national religion; the people are Sunni Muslims of the Shafi'ite sect, one of the most liberal of Islamic sects. Religion is the backbone of the society and forms a strong governing force.

Population

Maldivians are a mixed race, a result of contact with the many seafaring civilisations of the past. Most notable are the Indian, Sri Lankan and Arabic influences. The population is around 280,000, of which about 25 percent live in Male'.

MONEY MATTERS

Currency

The local currency is the Maldivian *rufiyaa* (Rf). Each *rufiyaa* is divided into 100 *larees*. Notes come in denominations of Rf500, 100, 50, 20, 10, 5 and 2. Coins are in Rf2, and 50, 25, 10, 5, 2 and 1 *laree*. At press time, US$1 was equivalent to about Rf12.75. The US dollar is widely accepted in the Maldives.

Foreign currency can be exchanged for *rufiyaa* through banks, resorts and authorised money-changers in Male', but there are no automatic cash machines on the islands. Some shops in Male' will change US dollars for customers. There is no black market and no restrictions on the amount when changing cash or travellers' cheques. Change only what is necessary, however – the *rufiyaa* cannot be exchanged outside the Maldives. At most resorts, bills are charged to the room

Above: men leaving the Grand Mosque in Male'

account, which is payable by credit card or travellers' cheques, so there is little need for local currency.

Credit Cards

All major credit cards are accepted at resorts, and in big shops and restaurants in Male'. If you have any difficulties with your credit cards, contact one of the following offices:

Visa/MasterCard/JCB
(c/o Cyprea Travels)
25 Bodu Thakurufaanu Magu, Male'
Tel: 32-2451, fax: 32-3523

American Express
(c/o Universal Travels)
39 Orchid Magu, Male'
Tel: 31-0321, fax: 32-5695

Tipping

Tipping is not a rule as most resorts and restaurants add a service charge, but it is widely appreciated. There is no standard rate but US$1 is a reasonable amount for good service rendered.

Taxes

There is a daily bed tax of US$6 which is usually included in the price of your accommodation. For visitors leaving the Maldives, there is an airport tax of US$10.

GETTING AROUND

Airport Transfers

Most visitors to the Maldives come on pre-arranged package holidays that include transfers from the airport to the resorts. Transfers are usually made by speedboat *dhoni* and can take anything from 15 minutes to three hours. Transfers to more distant resorts are made by speedboat or seaplane. Transfers by seaplane go from the airport directly to your resort. If your flight arrives at night and you are making the connection by seaplane, you will have to spend the night at a hotel in Male' and then transfer to your resort the next morning.

You should verify the transfer arrangements and fees with your travel agent when booking. Confusion can sometimes arise at

the airport, especially at peak hours. If you are left stranded, approach the information desk at the airport for assistance. If you have arrived without any pre-arranged package deal, hop on a *dhoni* to Male' and check out the tour operators there.

By Dhoni

Inter-island transport is usually by motorised launches known as *dhonis*. Resorts have their own *dhonis* and speedboats, which provide transport for airport transfers, excursions and other needs. The bigger resorts often have a fleet of boats for hire. Costs can be high, though: as much as US$60 per hour plus fuel. A ticket on a passenger ferry between Male' and the airport costs Rf10. From Male', taxi-*dhonis* are available for hire along the waterfront. From here to the resorts, the charges vary with the distance. For example, expect to pay US$25 for a *dhoni* (per boat) to Kurumba Village, 25 minutes from Male'.

By Air

Island Aviation *(see page 91)* operates regular scheduled flights to distant atolls like Addu and Laamu. The average tourist is not likely to fly to any of these islands, unless it is to the Equatorial Village Resort on Addu Atoll. Transfers between Male' and most resorts can be arranged with the resort or one of the seaplane services *(see page 76)*.

HOURS AND HOLIDAYS

Business Hours

The Maldives operates a 5-day work week, with the weekend falling on Friday and Saturday. Official government office hours are 7.30am–2.30pm. Private businesses are open 8am–1.30pm and generally open on Saturdays as well. Shop hours are Saturday–Thursday 8am–11pm and Friday 2–11pm. Banks are open Sunday–Thursday 9am–1pm. Most offices and shops also close for a few minutes each day for prayers. Prayer times are around 5.30am, noon, 3pm, 6pm and 7pm. During *Ramadan*, the fasting month, office hours are shortened to 9am–1pm, while shops open later, about 11am and close from 6 to 8pm for dinner.

Public Holidays

Most of the public holidays in the Maldives are Islamic ones based on the lunar calendar. The most significant event of the year is the fasting month of *Ramadan* which falls 11 days earlier each year. The sighting of the new moon marks the end of the fasting month, and *Kuda Id* follows, with a big celebration marked by much feasting and rejoicing. Two months and 10 days later is the celebration of *Bodu Id* when those who can afford it depart for the *haj*, the holy pilgrimage to Mecca. The Islamic New Year and the Prophet Mohammed's birthday are also celebrated as holidays. The non-Islamic holidays are:

New Year's Day	1 January
Independence Day	26 July
Victory Day	3 November
Republic Day	11 November

ACCOMMODATION

Apart from the accommodation featured in the *Resorts* section *(see pages 19–41)*, the ones listed here also merit consideration. Price ranges indicated here are for a standard double room (with full board, unless otherwise stated) for one night during the high season (December to April):

$	=	under US$150
$$	=	US$151–US$200
$$$	=	US$201–US$250
$$$$	=	US$251–US$400
$$$$$	=	above US$400

North Male' Atoll

Full Moon Resort (Furana)
c/o Universal Enterprises,
39 Orchid Magu, Male'
Tel: 32-3080, fax: 32-2678
Resort tel: 44-2010, fax: 44-1979
e-mail: fullmoon@dhivehinet.net.mv
web: www.unisurf.com
Located 6 km (4 miles) north of the airport, this 5-star resort has 150 air-conditioned rooms and water bungalows with hot and cold desalinated water. There are 52 water bungalows built on stilts over the water on the secluded north side of this large island. The full range of water sports is available, and the resort has one of the largest swimming pools in the Maldives. Restaurants include a pizza outlet, and Western, barbecue, Mediterranean and Thai restaurants. Attracts a cosmopolitan crowd. $$$

Giravaru Island Resort
c/o Giravaru Male' Office,
Opera Building, Male'
Tel: 31-8422, fax: 31-8505
Resort tel: 44-0440, fax: 44-4818
e-mail: giravaru@dhivehinet.net.mv
A small island just 45 minutes by *dhoni* from the airport, Giravaru is a bit built up but nevertheless has real beach-island atmosphere. The lagoon is so enticing the tiny swimming pool hardly seems necessary. There are 66 deluxe rooms, each with satellite TV, minibar, hairdryer and en-suite bathroom with shower and plenty of hot water. There is one restaurant, a coffee shop and two bars. $$

Above: modes of transport, old and new

Helengeli

c/o Karanka Villa,
Bodu Thakurufaanu Magu, Male'
Tel: 32-8544, fax: 32-5150
Resort tel: 44-4615, fax: 44-2881
e-mail: engeli88@dhivehinet.net.mv
About 44 km (27 miles) or four hours by
dhoni from the airport, this pleasant resort
has accommodation in coral-stone bungalows with thatched roofs. It has an excellent house reef (over 2 km/1.2 miles long),
and the remote location on the northeast edge
of the atoll means that you almost never run
into another dive boat. The clientele is
mainly Swiss. *$*

Makunudu

c/o Sunland Travel,
04-01 STO Trade Centre, Male'
Tel: 32-4658, fax: 32-5543
Resort tel: 44-6464, fax: 44-6565
e-mail: makunudu@dhivehinet.net.mv
web: www.makunudu.com
A little over 38 km (23 miles) from the airport, this is a small resort for a mixed clientele of well-to-do Europeans. Containing just
36 beachfront bungalows hidden in lush,
tropical vegetation, Makunudu puts the
emphasis on peace and quiet. Holidays are
on an all-inclusive basis. A European chef
prepares delicious meals, which may be
taken in your room, and once a week a buffet of Maldivian food is laid on. Service and
attention to detail give this resort its first-
class ranking. *$$$$*

Meeru Island Resort

c/o Champa Trade & Travels,
Champa Building, Male'
Tel: 44-3157, fax: 44-5947
Resort tel: 44-3157, fax: 31-4150
e-mail: meeru@dhivehinet.net.mv
web: www.meeru.com
At 37 km (23 miles) from the airport (1 hour
by speedboat; 2½ hours by *dhoni*), Meeru
is on the eastern rim of the atoll and well
positioned for good diving. The 227 rooms
include honeymoon suites, water villas and
land villas as well as standard rooms. It has
a restaurant, two coffee shops and three bars.
A small on-site museum gives a glimpse of
the Maldivian lifestyle, and *dhoni* repair
takes place on the beach. A cheerful, laid-
back resort. *$*

Nakatchafushi Tourist Resort

c/o Universal Enterprises
39 Orchid Magu, Male'
Tel: 32-2971, fax: 32-2678
Resort tel: 44-3847, fax: 44-2665
e-mail: nakatcha@dhivehinet.net.mv
web: www.unisurf.com
At 24 km (15 miles) from the airport, this
resort has 51 air-conditioned bungalows with
thatched roofs. All bungalows have baths
with hot and cold desalinated water. The
island has a large lagoon that is perfect for
sailing, windsurfing and water-skiing.
Restaurants include a coffee shop, a grill
and Asian fare. The clientele is mainly
British and German. *$$*

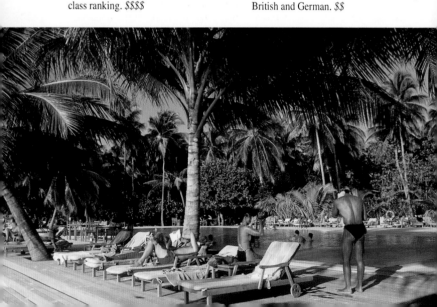

Paradise Island Resort (Lankan Finolhu)
c/o Villa Hotels,
3-04 STO Trade Centre, Male'
Tel: 31-6161, fax: 31-4565
Resort tel: 44-0011, fax: 44-0022
e-mail: paradise@dhivehinet.net.mv
web: www.villahotels-maldives.com
With 260 rooms (of which 40 are water bungalows with their own sun deck and stairs down into the lagoon) and only 15 minutes from the airport (10 km/6 miles away), Paradise is a major resort. It has five restaurants (two are at opposite ends of the island), five bars and coffee shops and the atmosphere of a busy tropical suburb. Rooms are well equipped and have satellite television. There is a beauty and hair salon as well as a gymnasium and fitness room. *$$$*

Thulaagiri
c/o H Jazeera,
15 Bodu Thakurufaanu Magu, Male'
Tel: 32-2844, fax: 32-1026
Resort tel: 44-5930, fax: 44-5939
e-mail: reserve@thulaagiri.com.mv
Some 20 minutes (13 km/8 miles) from the airport by speedboat, Thulaagiri was originally the first Club Med resort in the Maldives, but it is now locally owned. The resort has 58 Maldivian-style thatched-roof bungalows with air-conditioning and hot and cold desalinated water. There are fresh-water swimming pools along the beach. Well-known for its fine food, this resort serves breakfast, lunch and dinner buffets prepared by a European chef. Popular with Europeans and Japanese. *$$*

South Male' Atoll

Bolifushi
4th Floor, Alia Building, Male'
Tel: 31-7527, fax: 31-7529
Resort tel: 44-3517, fax: 44-5924
e-mail: gateway@dhivehinet.net.mv
Located just 12 km (7 miles) from the airport, the island of Bolifushi lies on the northwestern edge of South Male' Atoll. The diving and water sports facilities are excellent here, especially considering the very small size of the island. The 43 rooms are close together, but a holiday here is good value and the atmosphere is always laid back and friendly. *$*

Fihalhohi Tourist Resort
c/o Dhirham Travels and Chandling,
Faamudheyri Magu, Male'
Tel: 32-3369, fax: 32-4752
Resort tel: 44-2903, fax: 44-3803
e-mail: fiha@dhivehinet.net.mv
On the southwest edge of the atoll, 35 km (22 miles) from the airport, this resort has 92 thatched-roof beachfront rooms with views of its protected lagoon bordered by a coral reef. The island has an area of 8 hectares (20 acres), which means that much of the vegetation remains intact. Standard rooms have ceiling fan while superior rooms have ceiling fan and a mini-fridge. Deluxe rooms have air-conditioning, bath tub, hairdryer and room safe; all have telephones. Meals are buffets, sometimes served beachside. It is popular with families, mostly German. *$$*

Palm Tree Island (Veligandu Huraa)
c/o H. Athireegeaage,
Lotus Goalhi, PO Box 2014, Male'
Tel: 31-4008, fax: 32-7058
Resort tel: 44-3882, fax: 44-0009
e-mail: veli@veliganduhuraa.com
web: www.veliganduhuraa.com
About 30 minutes by speedboat from the airport, this resort has 56 bungalows with hot and cold desalinated water and individual terraces. The island is connected by a long boardwalk to the nearby resort of Dhigufinolhu. The shallow waters between these islands are ideal for snorkelling. The boardwalk has an open-air bar midway between the islands. Popular with European and Japanese tourists. *$$$*

Vaadhu Diving Paradise
c/o H Maarandhooge Irumatheebai, Male'
Tel: 32-5844, fax: 32-5846
Resort tel: 44-3976, fax: 44-3397
e-mail: vadoo@dhivehinet.net.mv
Located 8 km (5 miles) from the airport, this resort caters to Japanese divers and honeymooners. There is hot and cold desalinated water, air-conditioning and a choice of villas or water cottages/suites with private balconies. The luxurious water cottages feature a unique glass-top coffee table which lets you enjoy the multi-coloured fish swimming below. Vaadhu has an excellent house reef. *$$*

Left: the swimming pool at Meeru Island Resort

Ari Atoll

Ari Beach Resort (Diddhu Finolhu)

35 Bodu Thakurufaanu Magu, Male'
Tel: 32-1930, fax: 32-7355
Resort tel: 45-0513, fax: 45-0520
e-mail: aribeach@dhivehinet.net.mv
web: www.aribeach.com

Located 100 km (62 miles) from the airport, this long island has 141 rooms, both beachfront and over-water. There is a large lagoon for water sports (but no house reef) and a good windsurfing school. The main restaurant serves buffet meals and there is an *à la carte* coffee shop. Attracts a cosmopolitan crowd. *$ (half board)*

Bathala

c/o B.I.R. Hotel Management,
7th Floor, STO Aifaanu Building, Male'
Tel: 31-5236, fax: 31-5237
Resort tel: 45-0587, fax: 45-0558
e-mail: bir0587@dhivehinet.net.mv
web: www.aitkenspence.com/hotels

Situated on the northeast side of the atoll (48 km/30 miles from the airport), this resort is in a prime diving zone. Most of the guests are German or British divers, but if you come here for sunbathing and snorkelling alone you will not be disappointed. The beach is top-rate and the house reef one of the best. The 38 cabin-style cottages are more than satisfactory and so is the food. Good value for your dollar. *$*

Ellaidhoo Tourist Resort

c/o Travelin Maldives,
6th Floor, STO Aifaanu Building, Male'
Tel: 31-7717, fax: 31-4977
Resort tel: 45-0586, fax: 45-0514
e-mail: mail@travelin-maldives.com

Ellaidhoo, some 50 km (31 miles) from the airport, is centrally located in eastern Ari Atoll. The resort caters mainly to German divers and is reputed to have the best house reef in all of the Maldives. Nitrox training courses are available here. Guests can enjoy the reef and its colourful marine life without getting wet, through an underwater video camera connected to a television monitor set up in the bar. There is a main restaurant serving buffet meals and a coffee shop. All thatched bungalows are on the beach for the fresh ocean breezes. *$*

Halaveli Holiday Village

c/o EastInvest,
H. Akiri, Bodu Thakurufaanu Magu, Male'
Tel: 32-0850, fax: 32-3463
Resort tel: 45-0559, fax: 45-0564
e-mail: halaveli@dhivehinet.net.mv
web: www.halaveli.com

Halaveli is a lovely island surrounded by sandy beaches 62 km (38 miles) from Male'. An attractive feature of the 56 bungalows is that the surrounding vegetation ensures that each has its own private beach. The large lagoon is perfect for windsurfing, sailing, canoeing and other water sports. Halaveli Diving Centre is a PADI 5-star facility, and the Halaveli Wreck dive site is not far from the resort *(see page 66)*. All bungalows have hot and cold desalinated water and airconditioning. The buffet-restaurant serves a wide variety of dishes, often with an Italian twist, much appreciated by the mainly Italian clientele. *$$$*

Madoogali Resort

c/o H. Henveyruge,
Medhuziyaarai Magu, Male'
Tel: 31-7975, fax: 31-7974
Resort tel: 45-0581, fax: 45-0554
e-mail: madugali@dhivehinet.net.mv

Madoogali is found in northwest Ari Atoll, about 72 km (45 miles) from the airport. All rooms are thatched-roof bungalows with hot and cold desalinated water. Most of the usual water sports are available. The restaurant serves buffet meals with an emphasis on Italian dishes. The clientele is mainly Italian with some Austrian and German guests. *$$*

Twin Island (Maafushivaru)

c/o Universal Enterprises,
39 Orchid Magu, Male'
Tel: 32-3080, fax: 32-0274
Resort tel: 45-0596, fax: 45-0524
e-mail: sales@unisurf.com
web: www.unisurf.com

About 96 km (60 miles) from the airport, this resort has an uninhabited twin island, which is used for picnics. Nearby is the fishing village of Dhagathi *(see page 48)* and some of the best diving in the atoll. The resort has 32 air-conditioned bungalows, several of which are perched on the water. The clientele is mainly Italian. *$$*

Veligandu Island Resort
c/o H. Sea Coast,
Bodu Thakurufaanu Magu, Male'
Tel: 32-2432, fax: 32-4009
Resort tel: 45-0519, fax: 45-0648
e-mail: veli@dhivehinet.net.mv
web: www.veliganduisland.com
One of two resorts on Rasdhoo Atoll, just
north of Ari Atoll. There is a sense of being
away from it all here. It is a barefoot, anything goes kind of place, with a young management team intent on keeping everybody
happy. Veligandu actually means 'sandbank'
in Dhivehi and the beach-to-island ratio is
probably higher here than at any other resort.
The other draw is the hammerhead shark
viewing site nearby *(see page 66)*. The food
is good and the 63 rooms are comfortable. *$$*

Lhaviyani Atoll

Kuredu Island Resort
c/o Champa Trade & Travels,
Champa Building, Male'
Tel: 32-6545, fax: 32-6544
Resort tel: 23-0337, fax: 23-0332
e-mail: info@kuredu.com
web: www.kuredu.com
This long island was originally (in the 1970s)
a low-cost camping resort. It now has 300
rooms (refurbished in 1999) and has moved
slightly upmarket. With more than 3 km (2
miles) of white-sand beach and positioned
close to 48 diving sites, this resort is the
northernmost one in the Maldives, 40 min-
utes (129 km/80 miles) by seaplane from
the airport. It's popular with the young of
all ages and has a new free-form swimming
pool as well as a children's pool, six restau-
rants and five bars. *$$ (half board)*

Felidhoo Atoll

Alimatha Aquatic Resort
c/o Safari Tours,
Chandhani Magu, Male'
Tel: 32-3524, fax: 32-2516
e-mail: alidivebase@hotmail.com
About 48 km (30 miles) south of the airport, this is one of two resorts in Felidhoo
Atoll. It has 102 air-conditioned bungalows
with hot and desalinated water. The usual
water sports are offered, and the diving is
excellent. The clientele is South African,
German and Swiss. *$$*

Male' International Airport

Hulhule Island Hotel
PO Bag 20118, Male'
Tel: 33-0888, fax: 33-0777
e-mail: sales@hih.com.mv
This luxury, city-style hotel is on the air-
port island and can be reached by regular
shuttle bus from the airport. There is also a
free, scheduled *dhoni* service to and from
Male', so the hotel is popular with business
travellers as well as visitors in transit. Its
88 rooms are well appointed with every con-
ceivable necessity. There is a children's play-
ground, a water sports centre and a PADI dive
school, as well as swimming and wading
pools. With two bars, two à la carte restau-
rants and full buffet breakfast with Euro-
pean and Asian dishes included in the room
rate, it's almost as good as staying on a resort
island. *$ (bed and breakfast)*

Male'

If you want to stay a night or two in Male'
there are several hotels and guesthouses to
choose from. Accommodation is clean and
basic, with air-conditioning, hot water, TV
and direct-dial telephones usually available.
Day rooms for up to five people are available
for those with late-night flights. The price
categories indicated here are for a double
room, including tax and breakfast:

      $ = under US$55
      $$ = US$55–US$85

Hotels
Central Hotel
Rahdebai Magu
Tel: 31-7766, fax: 31-5383
e-mail: central@dhivehinet.net.mv
Just off Majeedhee Magu in the very centre of town, this is the newest and largest
hotel in town. The single rooms, double

Right: stylish accommodation

rooms, suites and apartments are all spacious and tastefully decorated. The hotel restaurant serves a wide selection of Western, Indian and Chinese food. Complimentary arrival and departure transport is included. *$$*

Kam Hotel
Ameer Ahmed Magu
Tel: 32-0611, fax: 32-0614
e-mail: kamhotel@dhivehinet.net.mv
This 29-room hotel, next door to the Relax Inn *(see below)*, is pleasantly decorated and has a small swimming pool that is perfect for an afternoon dip. There is a good Chinese and Western restaurant too. *$$*

Nasandhura Palace Hotel
Bodu Thakurufaanu Magu
Tel: 32-3380, fax: 32-0822
e-mail: nasndhra@dhivehinet.net.mv
Conveniently located, with a jetty just in front. The 31-room hotel has an 24-hour open-air coffee shop. *$$*

Guesthouses
There are many guesthouses in Male' offering rooms at lower prices. Some have air-conditioning and private showers, while those at the lower end may have shared bathrooms. Negotiate for lower rates, especially if you are staying for a few nights. Note that they are often fully booked by foreign workers.

Athamaa Palace
Majeedhee Magu
Tel: 31-3118, fax: 32-8828
This guesthouse has some of the most appealing accommodation in Male'. It has 15 pleasantly furnished rooms, with hot and cold baths and showers. The rooms come with balconies where you can watch the street activity below. Good Asian and Western restaurant on the ground floor. *$$*

Relax Inn
Henveiru, Ameer Ahmed Magu
Tel: 31-4531/2, fax: 31-4533
e-mail: relaxinn@dhivehinet.net.mv
Located behind the Nasandhura Palace Hotel, Relax Inn has 30 air-conditioned rooms with hot water, TV and direct-dial telephones. *$$*

HEALTH AND EMERGENCIES

Pharmacies
ADK Pharmacy
Majeedhee Magu, Male'
Tel: 32-7642

STO Pharmacy
Indira Gandhi Memorial Hospital
Tel: 32-3279, fax: 31-8563

Medical Services
ADK Hospital
Sosun Magu, Male'
Tel: 31-3553
This private hospital and clinic is fully staffed with its own laboratory and in-house pharmacy.

Indira Gandhi Memorial Hospital
Bodu Thakurufaanu Magu, Male'
Tel: 31-6647
This modern hospital was donated to the Maldives by the Indian government and is staffed by qualified Indian doctors.

Decompression Chambers
There are decompression chambers on 24-hour stand by, with full medical assistance, at Bandos and Kuramathi resorts. Emergency seaplane transfers can be arranged by

Above: Kam Hotel swimming pool

practical information

your resort and the clinics themselves. Travel and diving insurance is recommended because the costs of emergency transport and decompression therapy are very high.

Crime

In general, the Maldives is an extremely safe place for travellers. The crime rate is low, and the locals are generally courteous, but shy of foreigners.

Penalties for Maldivians doing things which tourists might consider innocuous (drinking alcohol, promiscuity, etc) are severe, so do not encourage them by irresponsible behaviour. The tourist can fly away, but the Maldivian could be banished to a remote island for several years or put under house arrest.

Police

The Maldivian police force – with their dark green uniforms – is the National Security Service guards. You will see them around on the streets of Male'.

Toilets

There are a few public toilets (fee Rf1) in Male'. One is down the lane beside the Emirates Airlines office on the waterfront Bodu Thakurufaanu Magu; another is near the fish market. Visitors can also try the toilets at the Nasandhura Palace Hotel and, while having some refreshment, at the Seagull Café off Chandhani Magu.

COMMUNICATIONS AND NEWS

Postal Services

The post office in Male' is located on Bodu Thakurufaanu Magu, beside the Nasandhura Palace Hotel. It is open weekdays 7.30am–12.30pm and 1.30–5.50pm. Airmail to Europe generally takes about a week to arrive. At the resorts, the front-desk staff will handle ordinary mail for guests.

Courier Services

All the major courier services as well as EMS Speedpost are available in Male'. If you are staying at a resort, the reception will make the necessary arrangements.

Media

The country's three daily newspapers all carry a section in English. TV Maldives broadcasts mainly in Dhivehi with some English programming. The English news is on at 9pm for 30 minutes. BBC and CNN broadcasts are available at the more upmarket resorts. The Voice of Maldives radio has two stations, with the English news at 6pm.

Telecommunications

The Dhiraagu telecommunications station is one of the most advanced in the region. Telex, fax and overseas telephone services are available at the station's office at the junction of Chandhani Magu and Fareedhee Magu (open weekdays 7.30am–8pm, weekends and public holidays 8am–6pm). Telephone cards are available in several denominations. Phone booths for international calls can be found outside the office. Direct-dial service is available at most upmarket resorts. The country code for the Maldives is 960. For Internet access there is a cyber café, run by Dhiraagu, on the waterfront, near the Bank of Maldives building.

LANGUAGE

Dhivehi, the national language, is derived from the Indo-Aryan language group and is related to ancient Sinhala from Sri Lanka. It contains many words of Sinhala and Urdu origin. The written form of Dhivehi is called *Thaana* and was introduced in the mid-15th century. It is written from right to left and contains 24 letters, nine of which are derived from Arabic notation. Accent marks above and below the letters indicate vowel sounds. English is widely spoken in Male' and at the resorts. You will hear a smattering of European languages and Japanese in tourist-frequented areas.

Useful Phrases

There are no words in Dhivehi for 'please' or 'hello' – a smile or gesture is enough. Here are some phrases you may want to use:
How are you? (informal 'hello') *kihineh?*
Goodbye *vakivelanee*
Thank you *shukuriyaa*
How much? *kihaa varakah*

What is your name? *kaleyge namakee kobaa?*
How old are you? *umurakee kobaa?*
What is your island? *kaley konrasheh?*
Where is the public toilet *faakhaanaa huree kon thaaku?*
Yes *aan*
No *noon*

USEFUL INFORMATION

Key Government Offices
Maldives Tourism Promotion Board
4th Floor, Bank of Maldives Building
Bodu Thakurufaanu Magu, Male'
Tel: 32-3228, fax: 32-3229
e-mail: mtpb@visitmaldives.com
web: www.visitmaldives.com

Department of Immigration
2nd Floor, Huravee Building
Ameer Ahmed Magu, Male'
Tel: 32-3913, fax: 32-0011

Local Travel Agencies
Crown Tours
H. Sea Coast, Bodu Thakurufaanu Magu,
PO Box 2034, Male'
Tel: 32-2432, fax: 31-2832
e-mail: ctours@dhivehinet.net.mv
web: www.crowntoursmaldives.com

Inner Maldives Pvt Ltd
H. Lady Bird, Kasthoori Magu, Male'
Tel: 31-5499, fax: 33-0884
e-mail: intermal@dhivehinet.net.mv
web: www.innermaldives.com.mv

Sunland Travels
04-01 STO Trade Centre,
Orchid Magu, Male'
Tel: 32-4658, fax: 32-5543
e-mail: sunland@dhivehinet.net.mv

Villa Travel & Tours
Ground Floor, 3/9 Star Building,
Fareedhee Magu, Male'
Tel: 33-0088, fax: 31-6731
e-mail: vilatrvl@dhivehinet.net.mv

Voyages Maldives
Narugis, Chandhani Magu, Male'
Tel: 32-3617, fax: 32-5336
e-mail: info@voyages.com.mv

Airline Offices
Air 2000, tel: 31-8459
Air Europe, tel: 31-8459
Air Tours International, tel: 31-8459
Balair, tel: 31-8459
Condor, tel: 32-3116
Emirates, tel: 31-5466
Eurofly, tel: 33-0088
Indian Airlines, tel: 31-0111

Above: Maldivian kids at school in Male'

Island Aviation, tel: 31-8758
Lauda Air Vienna, tel: 31-2980
LTU, tel: 31-2980
Malaysia Airlines, tel: 33-0088
Maldivian Air Taxi, tel: 31-5201
Martin Air Holland, tel: 33-0088
Monarch Airlines, tel: 32-3617
Singapore Airlines, tel: 31-4803
Sri Lankan Airlines, tel: 32-8456/32-0002
Trans Maldivian Airways, tel: 32-5708
Male' International Airport, tel: 32-2073
Male' Domestic Airport, tel: 32-2213

Tour Operators

In the UK the following tour operators offer holiday packages to the Maldives:
British Airways Holidays, tel: (0870) 242 4245; www.britishairways.com/holiday
Cosmos, tel: (0870) 901 0790 www.cosmos-holidays.co.uk
Cox & Kings, tel: (020) 7873 5000 www.coxandkings.co.uk
Distant Dreams, tel: (020) 8695 4950
Hayes & Jarvis, tel: (0870) 898 9890 www.hayesandjarvis.co.uk
Kuoni, tel: (01306) 747 002; www.kuoni.com
Maldive Travel, tel: (020) 7352 2246 www.maldivetravel.com

Useful Websites

www.visitmaldives.com
www.undp.org/missions/maldives
www.presidencymaldives.gov.mv
www.themaldives.com
www.travel.state.gov/maldives.html
www.maldives.com
www.inmaldives.com/pages
www.maldives.resorts.com
www.ipcs.org/projects/database/maldives.htm
www.worldskip.com/maldives
www.haveeru.com
www.lookmaldives.com.mv
www.dhivehinet.net
www.maldiveisle.com

Disabled Travellers

Because Maldives resorts are horizontal, a lot of walking, mostly on sand trails, is necessary to get around. So travellers with mobility problems have extra difficulties. However, there are wheelchairs available at the airport, and plenty of willing helpers to aid guests in and out of boats. Some resorts also have wheelchairs, as well as cement paths for getting around more easily. Among the resorts with facilities for disabled guests are Bandos, Kurumba Village, Paradise Island and Royal Island.

Children

Some resorts (particularly the more expensive ones) pride themselves on being 'child free' since they appeal mostly to couples and retirees. Families with children should head for the lower-priced resorts, which are generally more fun for the kids. Babysitting can be arranged in some of the resorts, notably Bandos and Kurumba Village. Children enjoy holidaying in the Maldives because there is no traffic and so much sand to play in, while teens will appreciate the resort discos, and the sports and diving.

FURTHER READING

The Maldives Islands: Monograph on the History, Archaeology and Epigraphy, by H. C.P. Bell. Colombo Printer, 1940.
Journey through Maldives, by Mohd Amin, Duncan Willetts and Peter Marshall. Camerapix Publishers, Nairobi, 1992.
Living Reefs of the Maldives, by Dr R.C. Anderson. Novelty Publishers, Male'.
The Maldive Mystery, by Thor Heyerdahl. Allen & Unwin, London, 1986.
A Man for all Islands: The Biography of Maumoon Abdul Gayoom, President of the Maldives, by Royston Ellis. Times Editions, Singapore, 1998.
A Hero In Time (a novel about Bodu Thakurufaan), by Royston Ellis. Times Editions, Singapore, 2001.

Right: some resorts are more child-friendly than others

INSIGHT
Pocket Guides

The travel guides that replace a tour guide - now better than ever with more listings and a fresh new design

Insight Pocket Guides pioneered a new approach to guidebooks, introducing the concept of the authors as "local hosts" who would provide readers with personal recommendations, just as they would give honest advice to a friend who came to stay. They also included a full-size pull-out map. Now, to cope with the needs of the 21st century, new editions in this growing series are being given a new look to make them more practical to use, and restaurant and hotel listings have been greatly expanded.

INSIGHT GUIDES

The world's largest collection of visual travel guides

Now in association with

ACKNOWLEDGEMENTS

Photography	
11	**AKG London**
25	**Courtesy of Angsana**
47, 48B, 70	**Andrew Forbes/CPA**
12T, 14	**David Henley/CPA**
2/3, 19,15, 19, 45T, 46T/B, 51, 52T, 80, 81, 87, 90, 7B, 91	**Adrian Neville/CPA**
5, 6B, 10, 18, 20T/B, 21, 23T/B, 24, 26T/B, 27, 28, 29, 30T/B, 31, 32T/B, 33, 35T/B, 36, 37T/B, 39T/B, 40, 41T/B, 43T/B, 44, 45B, 48T, 50, 52B, 53, 55T/B, 56T/B, 58, 59B, 61, 62T/B, 63T/B, 64T/B, 65, 66,67,68, 69, 71, 72, 73, 74, 77, 78, 79, 83, 84, 88	**Adrian Neville**
1, 7T, 8/9, 16, 49, 54, 60	**Didier Noirot**
12, 13, 15B, 57, 59T, 60T, 66, back cover	**Larry Tackett**
Front cover	**Steve Casimiro/Tony Stone Images**
Cartography	**Maria Randell**
Cover design	**Tanvir Virdee**

The updater of this edition would like to thank Inner Maldives Pte Ltd (www.innermaldives.com.mv) for their generous assistance with transfer and accommodation arrangements.

INDEX